WE

WERE

A

BAND

OF

BROTHERS

WE WERE A
BAND OF
BROTHERS

Captain Philip Heath, M.C. and bar

55th Trench Mortar Battery,
and 8th (Service) Battalion,
East Surrey Regiment

First published 2017 in the United Kingdom
by Brick Lane Publishing Limited,
London
www.bricklanepublishing.com
1

A catalogue record for this book is
available from the British Library

Paperback ISBN 978-0-9928863-5-6
eBook ISBN 978-0-9928863-6-3

CONTENTS

ACKNOWLEDGMENTS

The greater part of this book is devoted to my personal experiences in the First World War. I acknowledge with grateful thanks the help I have received from my old friend Lieutenant-Colonel Randolph Chell, who critiqued the manuscript.

Captain Philip Heath, M.C. and Bar

FOREWORD

A 'witch's brew [that] nearly blew our heads off,' is how Captain Philip Heath described breakfast at 55th Brigade headquarters in the latter stages of the First World War. It was a curry, the favourite fare of Brigadier-General Edward Wood for breakfast since his service in India. 'After a time I got to like it and, although the idea horrified me at first, I used to join the brigadier-general in his barbarous habit of breakfasting on it,' wrote Heath.

This and other anecdotes relating to the officers and men that Heath served with are a feature of the memoir he inked about his time on Western Front with the highly regarded 18th (Eastern) Division. His post-war words set out the life and times of a subaltern both in and behind the front-line trenches 1914–1918. It is a frequently harrowing, always honest and at times humorous account, first focusing on Heath's time with the 8th East Surreys and later the 55th Trench Mortar Battery.

Philip George Heath was born at Hampstead, Middlesex, in December 1895 to George Heath and his wife Martha Schmidt. He died aged 80 in September 1976 at St Marylebone, London. Heath was one of four brothers. Roland (1889–1975), John Moore (1891–1944) and Graham Douglas (1899–1969) also served in the First World War, whether in UK or abroad. Heath married Olga Sinclair in 1921. She died in 1986. They had twin sons, Peter Heath (1922–2002) and John Moore Heath (1922–2009).

Pre-war family life was comfortable for the young, somewhat shy Philip Heath, but early hopes of joining the Royal Engineers after preparatory schools at Guildford and Burnham and then Malvern College were soon replaced with a career in finance and international travel, presumably funded by his well-to-do father. For Heath, these early adventures marked the start of a life-long passion for travel and experiencing unfamiliar cultures.

Come the eve of the First World War in August 1914, Heath was back in London and working for insurance brokerage Messrs. Blackmore. Just shy of his nineteenth birthday, dark-haired, blue-eyed Heath was already fluent in spoken French, German and Italian. These languages would be the basis for his post-war career in insurance, much of which was spent abroad in Milan, Italy, supplemented with annual trips to France.

Like many young men of his era, Heath greeted the outbreak of war with enthusiasm. Here was a chance to fulfil his childhood dream of military service, to see some more of the world and to serve for King and Country alongside his friends. At this time, the reality of industrialised war was unimaginable to him. Eventually he was commissioned into the 8th East Surreys – thanks to an uncle, Major-General Sir Gerard Heath, who was Inspector of Recruiting in England – and began training prior to being sent on active service.

Heath would arrive in France in July 1915, and spend much of the next three-and-a-half years there and in Belgium, surviving the bloodlettings of the Somme,

Passchendaele and the One Hundred Days Offensive leading to the Armistice on 11 November 1918.

From his memoirs – reconstructed mostly from memory in the 1950s and 1960s, but drawing on wartime documents – one can chart the conversion of an optimistic, life-loving teenage recruit into a war-weary, cynical veteran. This is perhaps best seen in Heath's commentary following a day visit to Field Marshal Sir Douglas Haig's headquarters at Montreuil, although he never met the Commander-in-Chief. Of this visit to G.H.Q, he wrote:

> It was ... enough to enable me to begin to understand the utter lack of comprehension that existed between the High Command and the fighting troops, the key to all our losses and setbacks.

Such embittered sentiments were also evident in the memoirs, interviews and writings of other First World War veterans, although by no means all. Most commonly these were produced decades after the Armistice, and then following prolonged reflection upon their personal ordeals and sacrifices, and those of their friends and family killed or otherwise scarred by their trench service.

At the time, 1915–1918, Heath was more likely to have seized upon the obvious contrasts between his own and his men's dangerous, dirty existence in the trenches and that of staff officers in headquarters well behind the lines. It was this that he loosely touched on when referring to casualties in the 8th East Surreys and the 55th Trench Mortar Battery during their successful operations on the otherwise disastrous First Day of the Somme, on 1 July 1916:

> For two years they had lived, played, worked and trained together. Close friendships and deep affections had been created, so that, to me, and indeed to all the survivors of that battle, the sense of personal loss was almost unbearable.

Again, referring to his men during November 1916 at Regina Trench, also on the Somme:

> Their discipline, according to army standards, was deplorable and they dearly loved a chance of pulling the officer's leg. But I preferred it that way. We had been through the fire together, and had become comrades and friends.

And later, in the middle months of 1918, when reinforcements joined his trench-mortar battery but were as yet unproven and unknown to their fellow soldiers:

> The new officers and men were strangers to me and I cared little for them, whereas, in the old days, I had the feeling, which I believe was shared by the others, that we were a band of brothers so that every death in action of a man became a personal loss to us all.

With time these men, too, if they lived long enough and proved themselves, would join Heath's khaki clan. Those who failed to meet the implicit benchmarks risked becoming men alone, men unwanted by their units and even by a somewhat ruthless Heath himself:

All my new officers and men came from the infantry battalions of the [55th] brigade. I had a talk with all the four battalion commanders to explain what kind of men I needed. Their record of 'crimes' did not interest me at all, except of course for cases of cowardice. I was glad to have misfits, men who had got on the wrong side of their officers, or who could never get used to 'square bashing,' but they had to be strong, brave in battle and possessing of initiative. If unsuitable men were sent, they would be returned [to their battalions].

This last point was one on which Heath generally saw few shades of grey. On several occasions he either took or was about to take direct steps to have either soldiers or officers removed from his trench mortar battery, variously for clear-cut cases of cowardice, severe disciplinary breaches, poor conduct or general inefficiency and incompetence.

Yet, disciplinarian Heath was also experienced enough to identify that the strain of battle also took a toll on many men, and realised that more understanding solutions could often be found. He, for instance, might allocate exhausted soldiers additional fatigue work, send them for a spell in a rest camp, or give them jobs that limited the amount of time they spent in the actual front line. There were limits; men either unable or unwilling to pull their weight within the battery for any length of time were returned to their units. On other occasions, Heath confessed to highly unorthodox methods, to put it charitably. While under German shellfire at Schwaben

Redoubt, some men sheltering in a dugout began to show signs of shell shock.

> I had not the faintest notion as to how to set about the prevention of what seemed to be becoming a case of collective hysteria. In desperation, I picked up the handle of an entrenching tool and cracked it over the head of the first man with considerable force. ... It knocked the man unconscious and, when he came to a little later, he gave no more trouble.

Importantly, Heath very much recognised his own vulnerability to war weariness, shell shock, nervous collapse and the strain and responsibility of command. It is a point that his memoir makes repeatedly and abundantly clear. He first identified some of these factors in mid- to late-1916, and increasingly so by war's end.

Amid the 'grisly, chaotic nightmare' that was Schwaben Redoubt in the autumn of 1916, Heath said the he 'understood what it meant to be dead-and-alive.' Of his battery being committed to the fighting at Passchendaele in 1917, he commented that the 'prospect of the future holocausts in the Ypres Salient was far from inviting.'

On this note, Heath, like pretty much every other front-line soldier, had seen more than his fair share of war's horror. At Schwaben Redoubt he stepped gingerly along a length of trench 'crammed with corpses and bits of corpses'. He later penned this experience as a 'hideous nightmare' and added that 'hell can hold no terror' for anyone who had endured such ordeals in the trenches:

It was impossible to shave or wash. Food consisted of nothing but bully beef and biscuits. It began to rain again and this continued for most of the period, making the trenches almost impassable. Even in dry spells it was not easy to get along the main trenches, for the simple reason that corpses in various stages of decomposition lay along them in some places two or even three deep, and they stank to high Heaven.

Heath on several occasions came into close proximity with living enemy soldiers. He generally regarded enemy infantrymen and artillerymen as 'first-class troops who knew their business,' and appeared not to have held any overt animosity towards them, even after the death in battle of his friends and comrades. Fluent-German-speaker Heath conducted informal interrogations of prisoners on several occasions in the trenches, and on more than one occasion revealed compassion when tending wounded German soldiers:

He turned his head towards me and said very quietly: 'Ich bin blind, ich kann nicht sehen' (I am blind, I can't see). He leaned over towards me, and died in my arms.

Equally, Heath was quite prepared to end the lives of German soldiers in battle. He – in common with numerous other soldiers of the day – thought the business of killing to be 'barbarous,' but also saw it as 'necessary' to achieve both an Allied victory in the longer term, and more immediately secure his own survival and hoped-for return home to England. Regrettably, many never did get home.

In early August 1918, a young, well-liked subaltern was blown up in front of Heath, who found himself spattered with the man's gore. A few hours later, a deeply-shocked Heath reported to his brigadier-general, but had still not found time to clean away the blood:

> There I stood, struggling for speech, with my body trembling. I felt that I was just about out of control, and might burst into tears, or go crazy. ... I had felt for some time that I had spent too long in the front line and could not stand much more of it. I could still face danger, but it was becoming more and more of an effort. Previously I had often been terrified, like all fighting soldiers, but, knowing the necessity of mastering and concealing my fear, had usually, I hoped, been able to do so. But now I found that I had to force myself to leave the shelter of a dugout if shelling was taking place. My deepest private fear was that I might unexpectedly disgrace myself, and endanger the men I commanded, by breaking down or losing my head.

The brigadier-general gave Heath an hour to compose himself, which he managed to do. But it had become obvious to Heath and those around him that he was a tired man, potentially on the cusp of nervous collapse. He said his length of service and good reputation as a fighting subaltern saw him given the somewhat novel appointment of assistant brigade major of 55th Brigade, a position he held at the time of the Armistice. 'In all probability, it had simply been decided that I had done as much as could be expected, and was due for an easier and safer job, in spite of red tape,' he wrote. It was a decision that certainly preserved Heath's mental health, and quite possibly saved his life so that he might write this account.

Heath's memoir is a vivid and compelling insight to the First World War experiences of a long-serving subaltern. It is far from being just another khaki narrative studded with colourful accounts of battle, although it does have those, too. It is by turns harrowing and honest, and also occasionally humorous. There are plenty of tales about life on the Western Front, along with pen portraits of multiple officers and men that Heath encountered along the way. Also within the pages are numerous unguarded insights into his thinking, emotions and personality. One senses from Heath's often baroque lines that he found the process of writing his war experiences to be cathartic, allowing him to at least partially vanquish the ghosts and shadows of places such as the Somme and Passchendaele. *We Were a Band of Brothers* is the story of one man's war, but it could also be any man's and for that reason it is essential reading.

Andrew Macdonald, 2017

I

1914: Bank Clerk to Subaltern

At the outbreak of the First World War, I was a junior clerk in a City of London office, with a salary of £1 a week. To the ordinary Englishman the war came as a complete surprise. The murder of Archduke Franz Ferdinand of Austria and his wife, Sophie, Duchess of Hohenberg, had taken place only a month previously in Sarajevo and that this event was to be the immediate cause of a World War never occurred to ordinary people, who were quite unprepared psychologically for the ordeal before them. But there was no opposition to the idea. It was felt, amidst the sabre rattling and threats of the statesmen of the Triple Alliance, that Foreign Secretary Sir Edward Grey, had kept his head and done everything that an honourable man could do to avert the conflict. Lord Horatio Kitchener was appointed Secretary of State for War, and posters appeared all over the country with his great figure pointing at us and informing us that "Your King and Country Need You".

It seemed a matter of course to enlist, but this – for middle class, ex-public schoolboys such as myself – turned out to be more complicated a problem than it appeared at first. I was 18 years old. I knew nothing about military matters, except for the little I had

1

picked up in my school's Officer Training Corps. There were plenty of recruiting booths in London at which sergeants were busily shepherding men into Kitchener's Army, but the general opinion seemed to be that the war would be over before these men had completed their training. There remained the Territorials, who were already trained, and – as was a great attraction for boys such as myself – were already in uniform. Doubtless, as proved to be the case, they would soon be off to fight the Germans. Unfortunately, in any of the better known Territorial battalions, enlistment at that time seemed to be as easy as obtaining election to the Marylebone Cricket Club.

A friend in the office and I spent our lunch hours and evenings visiting the headquarters of the Honourable Artillery Company, the 1/28th (County of London) Battalion (Artists Rifles) and the 1/16th (County of London) Battalion (Queen's Westminster Rifles), where, beyond taking our names, they would have nothing to do with us.

The London Scottish refused me, in spite of the fictitious Scottish ancestry that I invented on the spur of the moment. In desperation, I even entered one of the Kitchener's Army recruiting booths. A sergeant looked at me (I am 6 feet and 2 inches in height), and said he thought I would make a likely recruit for a Guards' battalion. I took a poor view of this suggestion, as even I had heard of the rigours of life at Caterham, and, muttering that I would think it over, retired from the booth as quickly as I could.

After a week of these attempts to enlist, I happened to see a small advertisement that the 1/23rd (County of

London) Battalion, which was headquartered at Clapham Junction, had vacancies for a few good recruits. We visited the depot in our lunch hour and were accepted on the spot. We were given leave to break the news at the office but had to return the same evening. At the office the news was received philosophically. We two were the first volunteers from the firm and – to my delighted surprise, for I had only done four months' service at the company – the senior partner, a man who was by no way noted for his liberality, told us that we would be granted half pay for the duration of the war. Nowadays such an offer would hardly receive any thanks, but in those days you could buy a lot with 10 shillings, for example three bottles of whiskey, or 400 cigarettes. A private soldier's pay was only 7 shillings a week, so I was genuinely grateful for this quite unexpected largesse.

On returning to Clapham Junction, we were issued with one blanket each, and told that we had to sleep there. The depot merely consisted of a drill hall with no sleeping accommodation of any kind. I succeeded in getting hold of the lecture blackboard and spent a most uncomfortable night sleeping on this. Mercifully, next day somebody in command realised the futility of this procedure and for the next few days we were allowed to go home in the evenings.

During the next week we were issued with full uniform and equipment and were put through some intensive drill by the terrifying regimental sergeant major from the Guards' depot at Caterham. Then the whole battalion moved to St. Albans. Six of us were billeted in a small house near our battalion's headquarters in the County Hall. Thanks to our hostess, it turned out to be one of the worst billets I was ever to encounter throughout the war. The owner of the house was a pleasant and mild little bank manager, and he, together with his two schoolboy sons, were friendly enough. His wife, on the other hand, was a bad tempered avaricious virago. On our arrival we were greeted with voluble protests about the trouble we were causing, and the dirt that we would bring into her house.

The six of us were shown into a completely empty room, where we passed a comfortless night. The next morning, our hostess had had second thoughts. She had learned that she was to receive nine pence a night billeting money for each of us. For this reason, she rushed off to battalion headquarters and succeeded in having another four men billeted with her. Now there were ten of us living in a bedroom, which might have held four men in relative comfort, while the good lady was receiving seven shillings and six pence a night. This was far more than the rent for providing a whole villa. Throughout our stay she grumbled and did her best to make us uncomfortable, and charged us through the nose for anything that we happened to require.

In other respects I enjoyed life at St. Albans. Every day we marched out into the surrounding country for training. In the evening there was the choice between a visit to an excellent soldiers' club founded by the good people of St. Albans, and dalliance with the local shop girls. The way the latter carried on was an eye-opener to me, and their popularity with the soldiers was hardly a matter for surprise.

The 1/23rd London Regiment had the makings of a very fine battalion. The colonel was an extremely blue-blooded peer of the realm who was addicted to delivering patriotic harangues to the men. His effect on them was small for – two months after the battalion arrived in France – he became ill and relinquished his command. The officers, at least those with whom I came in contact, were a first-rate lot. Most of them had given up their peace-time holidays to training with the territorials so there was no doubt about their keenness and relative competence. Like their men, they possessed a civilian mentality, and, while not lacking in intelligence, had not acquired the rigidity of outlook and lack of imagination that characterised so many of the Regular Army officers. My company commander, Captain Vivian Wilkins, was an outstanding officer. During training he cheerfully shared in all the discomforts of his men, with whom he was very popular, although he took his duties almost too seriously. He kept strict discipline without nagging us, and there was little "crime" in his company. He was severely wounded at Givenchy in 1915. I visited him around that time in hospital and he seemed very pleased to see me and he impressed me deeply, for never have I met a man so full of the simple spirit of patriotism. The fact that he would be a cripple for life worried him not at all. The only thing that mattered to him was to win the war and he was supremely confident of this, provided that the junior officers did their duty, which was to dedicate themselves to caring for their men. Then, he believed, victory was inevitable for there was nothing that the British soldier could not do, if only he was properly led.

I had never met anyone like the men in my company. Apart from three or four ex-public schoolboys, they were a fairly rough crowd, Thames bargees, workmen and factory hands from the Clapham district. Their language was lurid, and most of them were extremely light fingered. At the start, the various articles in my kit kept disappearing in the most extraordinary way, but the same phenomenon seemed to be occurring to many others. I soon learned a simple remedy: if your mess tin disappeared, you merely pinched your neighbour's. Even if he found out, there were no hard feelings. I liked the men for their cheerfulness and for the genuine kindness with which they treated me, for they often went out of their way to show me the ropes and make life easier for me. In return, I became a sort of unofficial scribe for many of them who were almost illiterate. They would tell me, more or less, what they wanted to say to their girls, or to Mum and Dad. I would write the letter in a style that, after a time, became almost standardised, and would conclude with the ritual S.W.A.K. (Sealed With A Kiss).

On one occasion I very nearly ran into serious trouble with one of them. We had been sent on battalion training for a few days at Braintree, in Essex, and eight of us were billeted with a dear old lady, the widow of the local shoemaker. Her granddaughter, an extremely pretty girl, lived with her, and the two women mothered us and spoiled us, darning our socks, and filling us up with high teas and cocoa. One evening, Private John Fisher, an elderly ex-bargee, came into the kitchen where we were all sitting, obviously much too full of beer. On his way in he had noticed a rather battered top hat hanging in the hall, which the old lady's late husband had worn for his church-going. So, old Fisher with his paunch and black walrus moustache in his ordinary uniform, but with the topper perched on his head, made a somewhat unsteady entrance and stood, swaying in the middle of the kitchen. Then he solemnly raised his hand in benediction: "My friends," he said, "Gor blimey." Here the inspiration for the sermon that he no doubt intended to preach to us dried up, and he stumbled over, amidst roars of laughter from the audience, to sit down next to the granddaughter. Unfortunately, he did not leave it at that but began to paw her. Nobody moved, and I began to feel extremely angry. The only thing that occurred to me was to hit him hard, whatever the consequences. Fortunately, the old lady saw everything and acted before I could make a fool of myself. She went over to old Fisher, and took his arm, and simply said: "John, my boy, you are not well, I think you had better go to bed." He staggered out of the room with her, quite quietly, his topper falling off on the way.

During our stay at St. Albans, two notable parades took place, one pleasant, the other very much the reverse.

The first was a parade for an inspection by Field Marshal Frederick Roberts. The old gentleman, well over 80 years of age and in full Field Marshal's uniform, did his job as it should be done. He missed out nobody, and walked round the ranks, stopping from time to time, to commend the appearance of some soldier. Then he made a short speech praising the bearing of the battalion and wishing it Godspeed in the task that lay before it. We gave him three cheers and as he left the parade ground the regimental band played *Old Lang Syne*. It was the last parade ever to be attended in England by this fine old soldier for he died a month later, when visiting his beloved Indian troops in France.

The other parade was a very different affair. One of the sergeants had been caught red-handed stealing a valuable watch belonging to another sergeant. I do not pretend to know whether what followed was in accordance with the King's regulations, but I doubt whether such a thing would be allowed today. The battalion formed up in hollow square formation, and the sergeant, with his escort, was led into the centre. An officer read out an account of what he had done. There was a roll of the drums and the Regimental Sergeant Major stepped up to him and tore the sergeant's stripes off his tunic. Then to the strains of the *Rogues' March*, the wretched man and his escort left the parade ground to where a civilian police guard was waiting for him. It was a very ugly sight.

The new recruits, 200 in all, fired their rifle-training course on the range at Purfleet, Essex. In those days, Purfleet was almost uninhabited marshland, so, during the week of the course, we were billeted at Barking, two stations up the line. My host was an assistant in a grocer's shop. I and my friend slept in his parlour, and he and his wife were touchingly kind to us. The army provided an allowance of one shilling and nine pence a day for full board, but we had the utmost difficulty in persuading them to accept it in return for the excellent meals that they provided for us. I soon became an expert in bathing the baby and putting the other two children to bed. On the day we left, all the family embraced us, and the grocer produced a parcel for each of us with the label: "Something from the shop and only to be opened on the train." It turned out to be half a pound of tobacco apiece. When we paraded to march to the station there was a crowd of these warm-hearted people of Barking, kissing their guests goodbye, waving union jacks and cheering lustily as we moved off. Never have I met such a kind, decent lot of people as the inhabitants of Barking in 1914.

One day in November, I was summoned to the orderly room. There to my bewilderment I was informed that I had been granted a commission and was now a Temporary Second-Lieutenant. I was presented with a leave warrant for three days, and told to report to the 8th (Service) Battalion, The East Surrey Regiment, at a village called Aveley in Essex. My pay was to be 12 shillings and six pence a day, and a credit of £50 had been opened for me at Cox's Bank so that I could buy my uniform and kit. The adjutant shook hands with me and wished me luck. I learned afterwards that an elderly cousin of mine, a major-general at the War Office, was Director of Military Training, and was responsible for the appointment of all the subalterns in the army. Someone had mentioned my name to him, and I got my commission. It was as simple as that. In those days you were merely given your commission and told to get on with it. If you were completely incapable you were slung out and returned to the ranks.

I was sorry to leave my friends in C Company of the 1/23rd London Regiment. Many of them were killed at the battle of Givenchy, which was their first engagement. They did their best and fought very bravely, but owing to bad generalship and planning, they hadn't a chance of making a real success of it.

II

A Note on the 18th (Eastern) Division

Until 1917, each infantry brigade was composed of four battalions, with three brigades and a pioneer battalion, together with artillery and other services in a single division. The front in France and Belgium was covered by three armies in 1915, five in 1916 and 1917 and four again in 1918. The number of Army Corps in each Army varied according to the intensity of the operations being carried on in the Army area. The divisions forming each Corps were continually changing, as and when reliefs and reinforcements became necessary. But, except for the changes that occurred in 1917, when the number of infantry battalions in a brigade was reduced from four to three, the composition of the divisions never altered. My new battalion, the 8th East Surreys, formed part of the 55th Brigade in the 18th (Eastern) Division.

As a result of this system, while *esprit de corps* in the literal sense was completely non-existent, *esprit de division* was a very real thing. In the British Expeditionary Force the reputation of each division soon became known according to the qualities that it displayed in action. Without a shadow of doubt the 18th (Eastern) Division, in which I had the honour to serve, from the beginning of its active service in 1915 until the Armistice in November 1918, was one of the finest divisions that ever formed part of the British army.

The 18th was part of what was known as K2,[1] or the second hundred thousand men of Kitchener's Army. It was composed entirely of volunteers, until conscription was introduced in 1917. With a few exceptions none of the officers and men had had any experience whatever of army life at the time of their enlistment. Again and again they met and defeated the flower of the German Army, often under appalling conditions, and, at the time of the Armistice, had their opponents completely on the run.

In their first great assault, the opening of the Somme battle on 1 July 1916, the 18th was one of several divisions at the southern end of the British line that performed well. In September 1916, the 18th captured and held Thiepval and the Schwaben Redoubt, which was well known to be a strongly-fortified and tactically-important German position. It was in the front line, near the junction of the British and French Armies, when the Germans launched their great offensive on 21 March 1918. The division fought continually throughout the retreat and, after three weeks' continuous fighting, the exhausted survivors were part of the force that held the Germans at their furthest point of advance, Villers-Bretonneux, and stopped them from cutting the Calais–Amiens–Paris railway. The division was part of the attacking force on the Somme on 8 August 1918, a

---

1   K1 refers to the first 100,000 volunteers to Kitchener's Army, with K2 being the second 100,000 enlistments.

battle that was described by General Erich Ludendorff, who was Quartermaster General of the German army, as a "black day". It then fought continuously, except for one week's spell of rest, until the Armistice, chasing the Germans from the River Ancre to the Belgian frontier.

During the 1914–18 war, censorship meant newspapers were not allowed to mention the numbers of the divisions engaged in action, so as not to give information to the enemy, as if the latter didn't know! In spite of this, the press kept the public very fully informed as to the goings-on of the 51st Highland Division and the Guards Division. As for the Canadians, Australians and other Empire troops, there were times when a reader of the newspapers might well believe that English troops were taking no part in the war. We were all constant newspaper readers at the front. During the whole period I can only remember one solitary reference to the 18th (Eastern) Division. After the Armistice, we hoped, not without reason, that we might be chosen to take part in the Watch on the Rhine. The authorities thought otherwise. Until demobilisation, the division was kept on the desolate Somme battlefields, clearing the ground of unexploded shells and barbed wire – sustaining numerous additional casualties in the process.

But if the British public knew little and cared less about the old 18th, its survivors have not forgotten each other today, 50 years afterwards. Throughout its entire existence, the 18th only had two commanders, Major-General Sir Ivor Maxse until 1917 when he was promoted to lieutenant-general and appointed to command the XVIII Corps, and Major-General Sir Richard Lee from

1917 until the Armistice. Maxse was a remarkable general. Without a doubt, the 18th owed much of its success in battle to the manner in which he trained it. At the outbreak of the war, he was a brigadier-general and had led the 1st Guards Brigade through the retreat from Mons. He was then promoted to the rank of major-general and appointed to the command of the 18th. Before I had seen him, I asked one of our officers what he looked like. "Just like a bad-tempered bulldog," was the reply, which could not have been more accurate. He has mellowed a great deal since 1914, but he still resembles a bulldog.

His methods – and language – were all his own. Once, in the 18th's early days, he held an officer's conference in the open air. On his arrival, the officers stood to attention and saluted smartly. "Good morning, gentlemen," began the general in a genial way. "And good morning that gentleman there," he suddenly roared, having noticed one subaltern who was not standing to attention, but was leaning against a tree with his hands in his pockets. For the next five minutes Maxse proceeded to tell the unfortunate subaltern exactly what he thought of his appearance, habits and behaviour. Never before or since have I heard such a masterly dressing-down. His lectures – full of strange oaths and modern instances – were unforgettable. He would start explaining some tactical problem, chalking up signs on the blackboard to illustrate his meaning. Everything seemed simple and straightforward. Suddenly, he would glance at us: "And that, gentlemen, is all b--- b---. That's not what I want." He would then expose the fallacies in which he had been indulging and start away again. He was much more than a great tactician, for, in spite of his gruff methods, (it was not for nothing that he was known as the "the black man" throughout the division), he was intensely human and knew all about the British soldier's virtues and weaknesses, and how to get the best out of him.

A great stickler for service discipline, he often used to be found in a selected observation position, watching one of his brigades on the march and would greet every officer, as he passed him, by his surname, never making a mistake. It is probable that much of the credit for this feat of memory was due to his famous G.S.O.1. (General Staff Officer, Grade 1), Lieutenant-Colonel Bernard Montgomery, who later became Field Marshal Bernard Montgomery, 1st Viscount Montgomery of Alamein. Psychologically, it was a very shrewd idea, for it improved the self-esteem of the subalterns to find that the divisional commander knew them by name.

III

The Monotony of Training

When I reported for duty with the 8th East Surreys, they were living in conditions that were a disgrace to the country. In the middle of November 1914, in bitterly cold rainy weather, they were under canvas, 12 men to a tent, and another month was to go by before they were moved to better quarters. The food, though plentiful, was badly cooked, not unnaturally seeing that the cooking was carried out more or less in the open air. The camp was in Belhus Park, Aveley, and the ground, owing to the rain and perpetual trampling of the men, was like a quagmire. The nearest village was three miles away, so, except for the dubious amenities afforded by a recreation marquee and a wet canteen, there was nothing for the men to do when off duty.

The officers were a little better off. There was a tent for every two officers, and the officers mess was catered for very efficiently, under the circumstances, by Messrs. Nuthall of Kingston, who supplemented the army rations and fed us quite well in exchange for a daily contribution of three shillings from each officer. They even provided a major-domo (chief steward of a large household), a fat, little Mr. Quirk, who invariably appeared for work in a civilian morning coat.

In spite of the fact that the country had been at war for over three months, only two khaki uniforms for each platoon of 50 men had been issued. They were never used for ordinary work, but were handed out at weekends to men who had obtained leave passes. The officers and warrant officers were in khaki, bought with their equipment allowance, but the rank and file were dressed in blue-serge civilian suits, made of cheap shiny material, quite useless for protecting their unfortunate wearers from the bitter cold. On their heads the men wore blue forage caps with red piping, similar in shape to those worn nowadays by the Boys' Brigade.

The armaments of the battalion consisted of two ancient rifles, which had seen service in the Boer War, for each platoon. These were for demonstration purposes only. For drill, the men were provided with pieces of wood shaped like a rifle. Several of the subalterns had only arrived a few days before me. For the first fortnight we had to parade in a sort of awkward squad within a few yards of the rest of the battalion to be drilled by the regimental sergeant major.

The colonel was a pleasant but colourless old man. He was far too old for such a job and some months later, retired to his native Cheltenham. The company commanders were "dug outs," which meant their knowledge of all that makes up Army life was comprehensive. Their minds were far too rigid to understand the mentality of the new type of recruit that they had to train. Still, they did their best. They, too, left the battalion before it went to France.

The adjutant, Captain Alfred Irwin, was also a regular officer, but of a very different type. He, more than anyone, was responsible for turning this mob of civilians into a first-class fighting battalion in less than a year. Irwin had served in India with the 2nd Battalion of the East Surrey Regiment, and was on leave in England when war broke out. He served in the 8th East Surreys throughout the war, was wounded twice, and ended up as lieutenant-colonel, having been awarded the D.S.O. and two bars. He was the very finest type of British soldier, young, good looking, and bred with a fanatical sense of duty. His only weakness was a certain rigidity of mind, and it took a long time before he realised that he was dealing with enthusiastic civilians and not regular soldiers. During our time in England, I, frankly, detested him. He seemed to despise all the new officers (as was probably indeed the case) and was forever singling me out on parade, because a button was undone, or because my puttees were not rolled to his taste. When we got to France, he seemed to be a different man. His standards were as strict as ever, not for buttons and ties, but for efficiency. Provided you did your best, he became your friend, and none could have had a better one.

The junior officers of the 8th East Surreys, and of all the K1 and K2 armies, constituted the real elite of the country. Most of them were public schoolboys, among them many scholars. A few were older men, schoolmasters, businessmen and the like. Very few of them knew anything about soldiering except for what they had picked up at the Officer Training Corps summer camps of their schools. It did not take them long to learn the fairly simple technical side of the work. On the other hand, most of them had an instinctive knowledge of how to treat the men under their command. In those days people seemed to live much more in the country than they do today, and in the country villages, although there was a sharp distinction between the gentry and the villagers, the feeling was on the whole very understanding and friendly. This relationship carried over with these new armies. The young officers treated their men as friends and human beings, and did their best to look after them. In return, the men seemed to like and respect their officers, and certainly gave them their willing obedience.

The 18th (Eastern) Division was made up of Home Counties' battalions, namely the 8th East Surreys, 7th (Service) Battalion, The Queen's (Royal West Surrey Regiment), 7th (Service) Battalion, The Queen's Own (Royal West Kent Regiment) and the 7th (Service) Battalion, The Buffs (East Kent Regiment) in the 55th Brigade, and so on and so forth.

Presumably the lists of recruits had been mixed up. It is a fact that in the 8th East Surreys, nearly all the A company men were Londoners, those of B Company a mixed lot, nearly all the C Company men came from Suffolk, and those of D Company were Welsh miners. These men all had a great feeling for their own localities, and there were many groups of friends from the same village. They had enlisted in the belief that they would be serving in their own local regiments. When they discovered what had happened there was nearly a mutiny, but they soon settled down.

After a few days on the square under the regimental sergeant major, I was given the command of No. 9 platoon of C Company. With a few exceptions they were all Suffolk countrymen, farm hands, horse-men and so on. They spoke a broad dialect that took me some time to understand, never having been in Suffolk. Some of them were almost illiterate. They moved slowly and deliberately, and it took a long time to get ideas into their heads, although once these ideas were understood, they were remembered. On the other hand, they knew a great many things that I did not, such as how to get about country at night without noise, how to put up a shelter quickly, and how to manage horses. They had fine, strong bodies that they knew how to look after. They could walk for miles carrying heavy weights. They seldom grumbled. They would work extremely hard, if properly handled. They were clean, good-tempered and extremely brave when they went into action.

My platoon sergeant was a museum piece, an ancient reservist with a V.C., the only ranker in the whole of the regiment at that time possessing this distinction. Although the men treated him with awe, he was fairly incompetent, and, after a few months, retired from the army to the more peaceful vocation of Beefeater at the Tower of London. His successor, Sergeant Howard, although he was a native of Suffolk, was entirely different in character. Full of life and energy, he used to chase the men, but always with good humour. They liked him. After a time I began to get very fond of them all. I did my best with them. As time went on they appeared to be improving steadily in smartness and efficiency, although I fear my methods were at times most unorthodox and would certainly not have met with approval in the Regular Army. During the first parade at which I was alone with them, I told them that I knew no more about the business in hand than they did, but that I wanted to learn it as quickly as possible. This would explain why they would sometimes see me consulting the drill book while I was drilling them. I added that, while I was sure to make many mistakes, I would do my best for them on and off parade, and that I hoped they would do the same for me. In this way No. 9 platoon, I was quite certain, would become the best in the battalion. It was extremely naive on my part to talk like this, although I meant what I said. My excuse must be that I was only 18 years old at the time, and had never before had any experience of this kind. Nevertheless, I turned out to be a true prophet.

My company commander, after the departure of the "dug outs," was a young Old Wykehamist (Winchester College), extremely clever and efficient. But, he had the superior manner that seems to afflict so many Old Wykehamists and so he was not particularly popular. Although we rubbed along together without too much friction, we never became really friendly. When we had been in France for several months and were resting out of the line, he came into the company's mess one evening in a slightly more genial frame of mind than usual: "I have been talking to the colonel about you and we both agreed that you are the worst officer in the battalion, but that your platoon is the best. We couldn't understand it?" I replied that I agreed with him absolutely and had often pondered on this mystery.

After a month of misery at Belhus Park, splashing in the mud, the battalion moved into a camp at Purfleet, three miles away. Conditions here were very different. The men slept in huts made of corrugated iron. They had plank beds, paillasses and plenty of blankets.

After a time, the men received their khaki uniforms. Then came a complete issue of a new-pattern, short Lee Enfield rifle, together with the Lewis machine guns, webbing equipment, and all the other oddments with which the British soldiers must be provided. To complete the battalion's material equipment, the transport wagons and limbers, horses and mules made their respective appearances. It took some time before the latter could be attached to the former; those mules were devilish brutes. In appearance they were very fine specimens, 14- or 15-hands in height. They had been shipped from Argentina and had never been trained to harness or anything else. Practically speaking they were wild animals and, at the start, they had to be roped and thrown before grooming could be carried out. One of them actually killed his groom on the first night of arrival. However, there were plenty of men in the battalion who were used to this kind of problem, and it was not long before the mules were under control.

The battalion's headquarters and company officers were all provided with horses. Among these there was one animal allotted to the old major who then commanded A Company. It was the joy of the whole battalion. For practical purposes it was an excellent horse, strong and well-built and good tempered. In colouring it was unique. It was piebald black and white, with an extremely pink behind, which a very short stump of a tail did very little to conceal. It was promptly christened Pickles, and was a subject of much unseemly mirth to the men. Someone even composed an excellent, though bawdy marching song about it. The verses, quite unprintable, were chiefly concerned with its genealogy

('Bred by a zebra out of a guinea pig'). It was wonderful to see A Company marching into camp led by the major seated stiffly on Pickles, pretending that he couldn't hear the rousing chorus going on behind him: "Wotcher, Pickles. Keep your tail up, Pickles."

This A Company major was noted for his flow of language. On one occasion, when the battalion was at the Purfleet rifle range, the major was in charge of the firing party while the officer controlling the target markers was a 40-year-old subaltern, Mitchell by name. He was a man with a brilliant brain, a University Don in civilian life. Communication between the targets and the butts was maintained by field telephones, but these were forever breaking down. When they did function, they considerably magnified the voice of the speaker. Something went wrong at the targets, and the major was transmitting a wonderful flow of profanity through his telephone. He paused for a moment for breath, removing his receiver from his ear, whereupon the cultured tones of old Mitchell came through, loud enough to be audible to the entire firing party: "I beg your pardon, Major, but I didn't quite hear, would you be kind enough to repeat what you said after the word 'bugger'?"

One of the most difficult jobs in any battalion is that of the padre, if only for the fact that he never knows exactly what he is supposed to do. A padre holds the rank of a Captain. He had the right to hold a Sunday church parade, which it was compulsory to attend in those days, except when the battalion was actually in the fighting line. The 8th East Surreys boasted two padres and would probably have got along very well without the services of either of them.

Captain Philip Heath

The Rev. L. was Church of England, a curate from the East End of London. He was a dreary, ignorant little man, humourless and exceedingly pompous. On one occasion a young subaltern in the mess, impatient about some trifling matter, prefaced his remarks with "Oh God," without any thought of giving offence. "Do not blaspheme in my presence, boy" said the padre, in dignified tones. No one said anything, but the padre got more than he bargained for. The next day he happened to go into Gravesend to do some shopping. On his return he came into the mess whereupon another subaltern, known for his caustic tongue, remarked in his high-pitched voice: "Well, Padre, did you see any nice tarts in Gravesend?" The Padre fled in confusion.

Later on, in France, The Rev. L. very nearly caused a mutiny. One Sunday morning, the battalion came down from the line, after a ten-day spell in the trenches. The relief had taken place at night, and the men arrived at their billets at 8 a.m., covered with dirt and exhausted from lack of sleep. The Padre, who had been staying comfortably at the transport, without ever going near the trenches, ordered church parade at 11 o'clock. Strictly speaking, he was within his rights, and nothing could be done about it. Somehow we managed to get the men on parade, as dirty and unshaven as when they had arrived three hours before, but, quite rightly, we and they were furious. They Padre duly conducted his service all by himself, while the battalion stood sullenly and without joining in the hymns or prayers. When we were retired from the line after the first spell of the Somme battle in July 1916, half of the surviving officers were sleeping in a dugout, utterly exhausted after their ordeal. This same deplorable little Padre entered the dug out a few hours later and began to regale us with stories of the terrible sights he had seen while burying the dead. Mercifully, someone had still sufficient energy to get up and kick him bodily out of the dugout. After this performance he was sent away as incompetent and unsuitable.

The other padre, the Roman Catholic one, was a very remarkable man in his way. Father A. was a Jesuit, extremely erudite, and the author of various theological works. He was a Fellow of Louvain University and, before the war, had been a lecturer in a Canadian University. He possessed an immense amount of charm, and was one of the most cynical men – on religion and everything else – that I have ever met. Not unnaturally, he and his Church of England brother in Christ detested one another, and it was not long before a feud broke out between them, in which the Rev. L. stood no chance whatever.

In the army every recruit, on enlistment has to state his religion, which is duly engraved on his identity disc for obvious reasons. Religion is not a subject of great interest to most British soldiers, and in an English battalion like the 8th East Surreys it was natural that most of the men declared themselves to be Church of England, attended the Church of England parade on Sunday and thought no more about it. At the beginning, there were very few Roman Catholics in the battalion and these duly attended their Sunday mass under Father A. The Rev. L. was far from popular with the men, for he did not know them or ever attempt to make friends with them. On the other hand, everyone liked the genial, friendly Father A. So, Father A., who was by no means fanatical about his calling, began a little proselytizing work among the men, purely to annoy his colleague. The result was that, as the Sundays went by, the Church of England parade became smaller and smaller, while the number of those attending Father A.'s mass became bigger and bigger. The commanding officer finally put a stop to these indecorous goings-on, on the grounds that the men had had quite enough time to make up their minds as to which religion they belonged. Father A., as was to be expected, flourished and was soon appointed senior Roman Catholic Chaplain of the division.

The battalion was extremely fortunate in their doctor, Captain Edward 'Gimmie' Gimson. He was easily the most popular of the officers, and he well deserved his popularity. Good-looking and sturdy, he was the kind of doctor who inspired confidence in his patients. He was an excellent physician and surgeon. During one battle, a man was brought to his aid post in the trenches with a terrible wound in his leg. Gimmie examined it and said quietly to the man, whom he knew personally: "Sorry, old chap, but I'm afraid that leg will have to come off. Would you care for me to do it here, or wait till you get back to Base Hospital?" The man replied: "Thanks for telling me the truth, Doc. I'd sooner you did the job." Gimmie amputated the leg, there and then in the dugout. He was also utterly fearless and was one of the first officers in the division to be awarded the D.S.O. Before the war he had been in practice at Witham in Essex. On one occasion the battalion passed through Witham in a train, which stopped there for a few minutes. The platform was packed with people; it looked as if most of the population of Witham had gathered to greet their well-beloved doctor.

Two days before Christmas 1914 I was involved in
an absurd incident of which the chief protagonist was
our company's bad man, a certain Private Cook. This
man had been an old lag before he joined the army and,
true to form, spent much of his time in the guardroom
on account of his drunkenness and general indiscipline.
On this occasion, most of C Company had been granted
Christmas' leave, and my company commander told
me to march the men to the station and to say a few
words there about upholding the battalion's reputation
by good behaviour and sobriety while they were away.
Private Cook was not one of the party going on leave;
as usual he was in the guardroom, where he was to
spend his Christmas. That was the idea. I marched the
men to the station in good time and delivered my little
homily. To my horror, it was received with a yell "'ear,
'ear, 'ooray!" I looked up. There on the bridge over the
railway was Private Cook cheering loudly, and making
rude remarks about the "bleeding officer." I learned
afterwards that he had waited until the sentry's back
was turned and simply walked out of the back door of
the guard hut and, seeing no reason why he should not
go on leave like the others, had set off to the station. On
the way he had called in at a public house, filled himself
up with beer. Then he was on the bridge, drunk as a lord
and completely upsetting the discipline and gravity of
C Company. I had no idea as to how to deal with the
situation. Luckily for me, Private Cook made a mistake.
Singing away happily he stumbled down the steps of
the bridge on to the platform, straight into the arms of
his old enemy, the provost sergeant. He was escorted
back to the guardroom where, as previously planned,

he spent Christmas, this time with a sentries on duty. Shortly afterwards he was thrown out of the army as an incorrigible, to the relief of all who knew him.

I enjoyed life at Purfleet. Training went on day after day – drill, physical training, rifle training, firing on the range, and field exercises. It gave one a great satisfaction to feel the steady improvement in the platoon's efficiency, and in one's own knowledge.

The lighter side of the life was good fun. Somebody had the idea of starting a Rugger team and the talent that was discovered was really sensational. There were five Welsh internationals, from D Company, a Cambridge Blue, his brother who had played scrum-half for Marlborough, the captain of Dover College, and two officers who had played for Dublin University. There were four other experienced players, although not quite of the same standard as the first ten. I managed to scrape into the team as the fifteenth man. We challenged our neighbours, the 7th West Kents, and beat them 37 points to three. Not many men in the battalion knew anything about the game of Rugger, so there were very few spectators at the kick-off, but the news of our treatment of the 7th West Kents spread and soon the entire battalion was on the side-lines, delightedly cheering us on. We played a few other matches and, not unnaturally, won them all with some ease.

A few lecturers made their appearance, usually cranky individuals who had succeeded in persuading the War Office of the value of their particular hobbies. One of them was an old man who had invented a new kind of infantry pack, which, according to him, would enable the soldier to carry half as much again as at present.

It was hardly a subject to arouse enthusiasm among the listeners. But the old chap had such a pleasant, naive personality that the lecture was quite successful. There was also a certain Colonel Ronald Campbell, an instructor with the British Physical Training and Bayonet School, who was let loose among the training battalions in order to improve their bayonet fighting by instilling hatred of the Germans into them. "Now men," he would scream, "remember the babies that the Huns slaughtered at Louvrain. ... Straight into his guts, (matching the words to a bayonet action on a straw dummy hanging on a gallows), in, twist, twist back, out again." He was a revolting individual, unlike one of his assistants, who turned out to be the famous boxer, former British featherweight boxing champion Jim Driscoll, who sparred a few rounds with our Sergeant Thomas Palmer, who in private life was Pedlar Palmer, another very well-known boxer of the time and former world bantamweight champion.

It may not be generally known that the outbreak of the war had hit the London stage scene very hard and it was not until later that the big shows, such as *The Bing Boys Are Here* and *Chu Chin Chow*, began to appear. Consequently, there was a good deal of unemployment lasting for several months, in the profession. Messrs. John Broadwood & Sons, the famous piano firm, came to the rescue by organising concert parties for the troops. There were five or six artists in each party, and they each received the sum of one guinea and expenses per performance, while the units erected the stage, supplied the piano and entertained the artists to dinner. The scheme was a great success. Some of the players were really first-rate artists who were genuinely keen to do their bit by entertaining the troops.

We had three of these concerts, and among the artists were Ruby Miller, of the well-known Gaiety Girls, Thorpe Bates, later in *The Maid of the Mountains*, Norah Blaney, a charming little girl, who sang and played the piano. She and cellist Gwen Farrar were a very well-known turn on the music halls. Norah was a real trouper. At one of our concerts one of the other girls was unable to appear owing to sudden illness, whereupon Norah, besides contributing her own part in the show, took on all the items of the sick girl, singing every song as previously arranged in the programme. At dinner in the mess before one of their concerts, I found myself next to an extremely fat, pale individual. I had much difficulty in getting a word out of him at all, and none of us could imagine what contribution he could possibly make to the programme. He turned out to be the famous Barclay Gammon, a very well-known Music Hall turn. He was a really brilliant entertainer and his film melodramas, in which he played the hero, the heroine, the villain and everybody else, brought down the house.

There were also some concerts for which the talent was provided solely by the battalion. Most of the songs at these concerts I had never heard before, and some were extremely good in their way. On the whole, the more sentimental the songs, the better the men liked them. There was one most popular ditty with the incredible refrain:

You can have another Sweet 'eart any day
But notta nuther Mother!

Sergeant Lane, of A Company, was one of the most popular performers on these occasions. He had been a warder at Dartmoor Prison and there were two or three men in the battalion who had obviously been under his care at different times. When they happened to cross his path they would grin sheepishly. He would pretend not to recognise them but a close observer would see the twinkle in his eye. His contributions at the concerts were always comic songs, which had a slight atmosphere about them of the underworld or prison life. His favourite, entitled *Can't stop* described the adventures of a thief. One verse showed what happened when he entered a shoe store and chatted with the assistant. Here is how it ended:

It's a very nice pair of shoes,
I know,
But I'll take them off, for they pinch
My toe,
Now I've pinched them,
So off I go,
Can't stop, can't stop, can't stop.

Captain Charles Place, O.C. of B Company, was another brilliant entertainer with his songs at the piano. It seems to me that the songs of the First World War were far superior to those of the 1939–1945 war, probably because their writers and composers took much more trouble over their work than the tin-pan alley merchants of more recent times. Most of the songs were simple, witty and gay with melodious tunes, usually syncopated, for in 1914 the rag-time craze was at its height. It is a great pity that so many of them are now forgotten.

Incidentally, *Tipperary* was never the battle song of the British army that it was popularly supposed to be. The men always sang on the march, but I, for one, never heard them sing that song.

The battalion owed a debt of gratitude to some members of the London Stock Exchange who presented the complete instruments for a fife and drum band, replete with silver bugles. There were plenty of men capable of playing them, and a first-class band was soon at work helping to keep the men cheerful during the long route marches.

When we of the 55th Brigade arrived at Colchester in April 1915 to join the rest of the division, I found that we had been allotted a camp of ancient bell tents. Their previous occupants had only moved out the same morning. They must have been an undisciplined mob, for they had left the tents in a filthy condition. I was just giving orders to my men to carry out a thorough clean-up when one of the camp orderlies came up to me. "I wonder if you happen to know, Sir", he said quietly, "the last mob in those tents had three deaths from meningitis." I marched my men away, informed my company commander and we went off to interview the camp commandant. This "dug out" colonel seemed quite surprised at the fuss we were making, but in the end we succeeded in obtaining fresh tents on a new site, but not before I had threatened to report the whole matter to divisional headquarters.

After some days in Colchester we marched to Ipswich and took part in a week's large-scale manoeuvres in the Hollesley Bay area. The last day was sheer torture. After a very heavy day chasing across open country we tramped into Ipswich, tired out, at 8 p.m. We settled the men in comfortable billets and inspected their dinners. Then came an order for the battalion to parade again at midnight to march to Colchester, 20 miles away. I shall never know how we accomplished that march without a single man falling out. Night marching is a far stiffer proposition than marching by day. And, as the result of manoeuvres day after day for days in the wild and rough common land of Hollesley Bay, the men and their boots were nearly worn out before they started the march. At midnight the battalion trudged off down the Colchester road, all the men sullen, some of them drunk. They were carrying full equipment and packs. All of them were doing their best, but as the hours crawled by it was obvious that some were very near exhaustion. It was grand to see the subalterns and senior non-commissioned officers easing their men along and helping the weaker ones by carrying their loads. I saw one brawny sergeant carrying two extra packs, besides his own. At 5.30 a.m. dawn was breaking. Just as I was wondering how we should ever manage another mile, a wonderful sight appeared – at the side of the road there were all our travelling cookers drawn up with tea and plenty of bacon, bread and jam for everybody. When the battalion started off again an hour later, in much better shape after their breakfast and rest, there was its band in the lead, playing non-stop for the last five miles. We must have been worth watching as we marched, at attention, past the guard on to the barrack-square. After dismissal from parade several of the men dropped on the ground where they had stood, fast asleep. They had covered 62 miles in the previous 48 hours in full marching order.

In May, the division moved once more and the 8th East Surreys found themselves in huts at Codford, a desolate spot on the Salisbury Plain. I hated the place. I have never seen a district so entirely without shade; it was a very hot summer and the sun blazed down pitilessly on the corrugated iron roofs of the huts. Day after day we scrambled over the bleak hills and, when we returned to camp, there was nothing whatsoever in the way of diversion.

I can only remember one comic incident that served to lighten this dreary period. During one of the innumerable field days, our company was lying in line on a chalk ridge. Although the time was 2.30 p.m., we had been on the move all the morning without any chance to eat our rations and had had nothing to eat or drink since our 7 a.m. breakfast. One of the items of training consisted in starting a message at one end of the line, and passing it from man to man by word of mouth. The message that arrived at the end of the line was usually completely different to the one that had been sent off. On this occasion the men on the left of the line could see a message being passed down and, not unnaturally, expected that it would be an order to fall out for rations. When it finally arrived, for once, in its correct form, it contained the stirring tidings, sent by the old second-in-command, that "Stony Hill has fallen." It was greeted with "raspberries" from the men. Suddenly, one of my men, without any warning, rolled over and over, 30–40 feet down the far slope of the ridge, landing motionless on his back. "What do you think is the matter with you?"

shouted my platoon sergeant. The man looked at him: "Over-eating, sergeant," he replied with simple dignity.

By this time the battalion had become first-class. Its drill and training were of a standard not far behind that of the best Regular Army units and in certain respects, such as initiative and lack of rigidity, it, and some other battalions of K2, might even have been considered superior. These New Armies were subject, at least in theory, to exactly the same code of discipline as that of the Regular Army, and this code is extremely rigid, and, in many ways, unnecessarily harsh. The slightest trivial offence constituted a "crime," a word that in civilian life has a grave meaning. For misdemeanours – such as being not properly shaved on parade, having a button undone, or failing to salute an officer – the offender was liable to be marched into the presence of the colonel in the orderly room, under escort. His cap was snatched off, in case he lost his temper and threw it at someone. After evidence had been given he was asked what he had to say, often remaining tongue-tied through nervousness. The colonel then pronounced judgment and sentence and the man was marched out, still under escort. The punishments for trivial crimes consisted of so many days C.B. (confined to barracks), fatigues, pack-drill and so on. For more serious offences, such as being absent without leave, the colonel could award up to 28-days field punishments No. 1. This consisted of confinement to the guard-room, innumerable drills and fatigues, and, in addition, the wretched culprit was tied up to a wagon for an hour a day, in full view of the other men.

Luckily the young officers shared, to a large degree, the civilian mentality of the men, and did their best to keep them out of trouble, provided that they were pulling their weight in the things that mattered. Consider, for example, the case of Private Bird in my platoon, who did not answer to his name on parade. I asked where he was. "Gone to 'ave a shave, zurr," said one of the men. Five minutes later, Bird appears, shaved and clean (a somewhat unusual occurrence), and elbows his way into the ranks. Now, I know Bird pretty well and rather like him. He is a dark, little man, smaller than the others, always grinning and very popular with the other men, who treat him as a mascot. They are for ever pulling his leg. He can hardly read or write, but possesses a considerable knowledge of country life, for he has always been a farm-labourer in Suffolk. He is slow in learning, but does not forget what he has learnt. Moreover in spite of his short stature, he never falls out on a march and always does his share of work. So I tell him not to be late in future, adding that it is a real treat to see him properly shaved, for a change, whereupon Bird grins amiably and the platoon marches off. But, after parade, I tell the platoon sergeant to get hold of two or three of Bird's mates and tell them to see that he appears on parade on time and properly shaved in the future.

If I had told the sergeant to take note of Private Bird's name on a charge, he would probably have received a trivial punishment, or even an admonition. He would have felt bitter about this, because he would have had no idea that he had committed what he considered to be a "crime." In his previous life, a delay of five minutes was neither here nor there. And, had he not gone off to the barber for a shave, which had cost him a quarter of a day's pay, merely to satisfy the officer who, on previous occasions, had criticised his efforts to shave himself? As a result, he would have committed more and more "crimes" and ended up as a bad, discontented soldier. That is a very small example of the way in which we subalterns dealt with our men, and the results were admirable. There was very little official "crime." Officers who behaved as friends to their men got far more out of them than if the rigid army code was strictly applied.

Towards the end of July, after a few days' final leave, the battalion entrained to Folkstone and sailing by night, in a collier, arrived next morning at Boulogne, in France.

No mention has been made of the new lieutenant-colonel, who took over the command of the battalion in May. At first sight, he seemed to be an ideal man for the post. About 40 years of age, he was good-looking, and a fine rider. He was obviously fully conversant with army technique and training, and displayed, on occasion, a great charm of manner. According to all accounts he was also a brave soldier, for he had been wounded at Festubert and had been awarded the D.S.O. for his conduct. Unfortunately, he and I, from the very start, did not hit it off. Obviously he did not like me; no doubt he had his reasons, although I never knew what these were. For my part, some instinct made me distrust him from the very beginning, and that might well be a very serious matter for me; on active service a colonel practically has powers of life and death over the officers and men of his command.

At the end of June 1915, I and seven other subalterns were summoned to the orderly room where the colonel treated us to a homily. It appeared that the battalion had too many subalterns. He had noticed that we subalterns were very slack in our work, and we should certainly be left behind in England when the battalion went to France, unless we quickly mended our ways. There was a good deal more to the same effect, couched in somewhat offensive language.

I was rather bewildered by all this. I knew that I was far from being a perfect officer. But, except during the first few weeks, I had escaped all serious rebukes, and I knew that my platoon was considered one of the best in the battalion. So, the same evening, I waited till the colonel went to his hut to go to bed, knocked on the door and asked if I could speak to him. I said that in reference to his talk, although I had no inflated opinion of myself, I was genuinely doing my best, was very keen to go to France with the battalion and therefore would he be good enough to explain my faults so that I could correct them? The colonel was charming. He said there was nothing seriously wrong, although my personal appearance on parade might, perhaps be improved upon. It was only as an afterthought that my name had been added to the list of officers to whom he had spoken that morning. He rose, patted my back and said, "Don't worry, my boy. You will be coming out with us to France all right," and away I went feeling much relieved.

Ten days later the same officers, with another for good measure, were summoned once more to see the colonel in the orderly room. The colonel was considerably more offensive than on the previous occasion. He said the battalion would embark for France on 27 July without us. Our destination would be the 11th (Reserve)

Battalion, East Surrey Regiment, which was then in process of being formed. We were then dismissed.

I stayed where I was and asked if I could speak to him. He replied that, if I were to try to make him alter his decision, it would be a waste of time for he had made up his mind. "No, Sir," I replied, "I understood that already. I only wanted to ask you if you could arrange for me to resign my commission." He looked somewhat surprised and asked my reasons. "I have been with this battalion nearly from the start," I said. "My one object was to go with it to France to fight the Germans. If I was sent to the 11th East Surreys, I should have to start again from the beginning and undergo nearly another year of training in a unit that I know nothing of and care for less. I am not going to do it, if I can possibly avoid it. If I am not fit to have command in this battalion, presumably I am not fit to have one anywhere else. If my request is granted, I promise I will immediately re-enlist in the ranks." After all the training I had had, it should not be difficult to be accepted for service in a battalion due for active service, even, perhaps, in this brigade. The colonel replied that he considered it a sporting offer, but doubted whether my idea was possible. He said he would see what he could do. Three days later, he took me aside in the mess. "It's alright," he said, "I have been able to arrange for you to come out with the battalion, after all." So that problem was settled, but the colonel and I had by no means finished with one another.

The train journey to Folkstone was marked by a pleasant little incident. The train stopped for a few minutes at Guildford. The platform was crowded with troops drawn up as if on parade, with a brass band on the flank. As our train stopped, the band struck up, the men broke their ranks and boarded the train with small gifts of cigarettes and the like for our men. The explanation was simple – and typical of the British Army at its best. Guildford was the headquarters of the Queen's West Surrey Regiment, sister regiment of the East Surreys. All the officers and men at the depot had come to the station to say goodbye and wish good luck to their comrades. The train moved out to the accompaniment of a roar of cheering and the band of the Queen's playing *A Southerly Wind and a Cloudy Sky*, which was the regimental march. It was a wonderful send off, and all the more heart-warming for being quite unexpected.

IV

In France

1915–1916

On arrival at Boulogne after an uneventful channel crossing the battalion spent a night in a camp on the hill, and entrained next day to Bertangles, a village several miles east of Amiens.

The way in which troops, British and French, were treated by the French Railways during the 1914–1918 war can only be described as disgraceful. The prevailing idea of the French authorities seemed to be that the transport of troops was a distasteful chore, to be carried out when they felt like it, provided, of course, that it did not upset the regular timetables. It went without saying that rolling stock, much of it looking as if it had been reclaimed from the scrap heap, was used for this purpose.

The men always travelled in goods trucks that bore the label: *8 chevaux, 40 hommes* (8 horses, 40 men). The officers travelled in dilapidated second-class, non-corridor carriages, in which the windows were broken and the upholstery was falling to bits. The trains never started punctually, so that it was quite normal that an entraining battalion should arrive at the station at the agreed time and then have to wait for three or four hours, often in the open and under steady rain, before the train put in an appearance. The trains crawled along at a snail's pace and had to give way to all civilian trains travelling under the civilian timetable. It is almost unbelievable, but on one occasion the battalion arrived at the station at the appropriate time and at its destination 22 hours later. The distance covered was exactly 23 miles! Nobody cared, and there was nothing that we could do about it.

After a few days at Bertangles the battalion marched to Dernancourt, a village four miles from the trenches. A few days later, the battalion performed its first spell of duty in the line. This was for instructional purposes only, for the troops of the 5th Division, who were in the trenches, remained where they were to show the newcomers the ropes. In the next spell, a proper relief was effected and the 8th East Surreys were left to their own resources in the front line. It was at Dernancourt that an absurd incident occurred, of which the now-promoted Major Alfred Irwin, second in command of the battalion, was one of the unwitting protagonists.

Several units called Labour Battalions had recently arrived in France to carry out such jobs as road making, ground levelling and so on. There were a few skilled men among them, but most of them were English navvies and unskilled labourers, with some real veterans. One old chap confided to me that he had given his age on enlistment as 50, but he was really 63. They were good, willing workers, and were always a source of good natured amusement to the Kitchener's Army men on account of their unorthodox, not to say eccentric, ways. Needless to say, discipline, as practised in the army, had no meaning for them.

One day, Major Irwin was strolling slowly up the main road of Dernancourt in earnest conversation with a high-ranking staff officer, the latter resplendent with his red tabs and gold-braid cap. Suddenly, Irwin felt a tap on his shoulder. Looking round, he found that his interlocutor was an old sweat from a Labour Battalion holding out a swagger stick. The latter remarked politely, "Oy, yer mate's dropped 'is cane," handed on the stick and calmly went on his way, leaving the two officers shaking with laughter.

The famous cartoonist Bruce Bairnsfather apparently got to hear of this, and used it as a subject of one of his best cartoons in the *Bystander*. Bairnsfather, the creator of the "Old Bill" series of illustrations, was a brilliant artist. He had a great sense of the comic, but he always laughed with and never at the army. The most famous of all his cartoons was the "Better 'Ole." It portrays "Old Bill," with his walrus moustache, ill-fitting uniform and cap comforter showing under his tin hat, crouching in a shell hole in the company of an extremely apprehensive new arrival. The caption: "Well, if you knows of a better 'ole, go to it."

The trenches that the 8th East Surreys took over were in the area between the River Ancre and the River Somme, opposite the remains of Fricourt village. They had been constructed by the French, and had only been taken over by the British a few weeks earlier.

The soil, chalk and sand were not unsuitable for digging dugouts, but the French had taken little advantage of this fact. Although warm and fairly roomy, most were situated too near the surface and were not properly shell-proofed. To warm them, the walls were covered in straw held in position by wire netting. This straw was the abode of hordes of field mice, pestilential little beasts that plagued us incessantly. Any scrap of food left open in the dugout was immediately fouled by them, thus causing a fair amount of disease. When a soldier came off sentry duty at night, it was not amusing, on putting out the stub of candle, to feel three or four of these little animals running up and down his body. Like everything else, we got used to it after a time, but one officer, after repeated nights of insomnia from this cause, broke down and had to be sent back to England. One of our sergeants, coming off duty, put on his woollen cap comforter, but took it off again rather quickly for, in his absence, three field mice had made themselves comfortable in it.

The trenches were also infested by rats, horrible fat, mangy brutes that lived on the scraps of food thrown out of the trenches by the men, and any carrion, human or otherwise, that they could find. At intervals, light bridges had been laid over the tops of the trenches. On quiet days we subalterns, with loaded revolvers, would lie in wait for the rats as they went across: I once killed one at a range of 14 yards, a far more difficult feat than it might appear to those unaccustomed to shooting at a moving target with a revolver.

There were also a few cats prowling around the trenches, which must have been left behind by the previous inhabitants of the ruined nearby villages. They were now practically wild animals, very large and savage, yowling horribly at night, and we hated them.

Feeding the troops sometimes presented a difficult problem. The food was brought up to battalion headquarters every night by the quartermaster's transport. One hot meal a day was cooked there, and this, if humanly possible, was carried up to the front line, in heat-retaining dishes together with the rations, by fatigue parties. Cooking in the open was forbidden in the front lines to avoid smoke showing, so the men brewed up their tea and heated up their tinned food with the aid of a so-called Tommy cooker, which was a type of compact, portable stove. These were small, round tins containing wax, steeped in paraffin. When the worst came to the worst, body and soul were kept together with cold bully beef and army biscuits. The latter were large, square objects, nearly tasteless and hard as nails.

Behind the front line trenches lay the support line, and behind the latter was the reserve line, where battalion headquarters was situated. Two companies manned the battalion's front line, while the other two were used for trench digging, fatigues and so on. Eight days more or less would be a normal tour of duty in the trenches. Very few front line sentries were needed, or posted by day, which was, as far as possible, the time for sleeping. At night, life in the trenches became very active. The sentries fired continuously across no-man's-land, and, from time to time, star shells were fired, the German variety being far superior in intensity to our own Verey lights, or flares. Fatigue parties came up with rations and material and there would be occasional wiring parties and patrols in no-man's-land. Working in no-man's-land was not as hazardous as it might appear, provided that the Germans did not spot you, because bullets fired at night always tend to fly high. But, any working party or patrol caught in the flare lights would consider itself lucky if it got back without casualties from the German machine guns. Men were taught to stand motionless if star shells were being fired to land in their vicinity. One night one was fired in my direction as I was working in no-man's-land. I duly stood still, but, to my horror, it seemed about to fall straight on top of me. That might well have meant my being burnt alive, for the shells were made of phosphorous and practically impossible to extinguish. Luckily for me, it missed me by six feet.

Patrolling was an extremely chancy business. Anything or nothing might happen. A patrol might be ordered to examine the German wire, or any suspicious sign of new digging. One's safety depended to a certain extent on skill in moving noiselessly, and in sense of direction, not to mention presence of mind if an enemy patrol was encountered. Several unpleasant things could happen to an unlucky patrol, death or wounds from machine guns, or capture by enemy patrols or through blundering into the German trenches.

The front lines were from 200–300 yards apart, except at one place on the right of the line called the Tambour Duclos, where the French had dug a large circular redoubt jutting out towards the German trench, at the nearest point only 40 yards away. It was a horrible, sinister place. Casualties were always occurring there because, owing to its shape, it was very vulnerable to artillery fire. But the worst feature of the Tambour was the mining, which was carried on by both sides by companies of professional miners with their picks and pit props. The aim was to dig the shaft so that it ran below the German line; a charge was then blown and artillery would be concentrated on the spot, presumably to disorganise the rescue parties and cause more casualties. It was a horrible barbarous business. We, of course, had listening apparatus; so had the Germans. Although we gradually got the upper hand, we by no means had it all our own way.

The result was that men on duty in the Tambour ran the risk of being blown up at any moment. One platoon of the 7th Buffs in our brigade was caught in this way on their second tour of duty in the line, and lost 21 men. The non-commissioned officers of the mining companies had first-aid apparatus and hot coffee always ready, to deal with casualties caused by the collapse of tunnels, or asphyxia from mine gas. The miners themselves used to carry with them canaries in small cages. Apparently the unfortunate canaries became susceptible to mine gas sooner than human beings and would then give warning of the danger by dying.

During one of the battalion's earlier spells in the trenches, I had another brush with the lieutenant-colonel. At one part of the line there were two small salients, about 150 yards apart, with their nearest points some 200 yards from the German front line. One afternoon in September 1915, I was told that Captain Charles Pearce, my company commander, wished to see me. He told me that the lieutenant-colonel had ordered that a new trench was to be dug to join up the front of the two salients and that my platoon was to dig it that same evening. He added almost as an afterthought that all nearby sentry posts and artillery had been warned about this working party, which would start operating at 8.00 p.m. I could feel myself trembling, for the order practically amounted to a death sentence for me and my platoon. At 8.00 p.m. visibility was still very nearly perfect. All the Germans would have to do would be to wait until we had climbed out of the front-line trench into no-man's-land and then turn a couple of machine guns on to us.

"Look here, Pearce," I said. "You are sure the order came from the colonel and not from you?" He assured me this was so. "In that case," I said, "you will, please, tell the colonel that, whatever the consequences may be, I refuse to carry out that order as it stands. If he wants to know the reason, it is that to order a platoon to walk into the middle of no-man's-land is sheer murder. I know that if he wants to have me killed, and gives me personally an order like this one, that is his privilege, and I have to obey. But, I am in charge of No. 9 platoon, and my job is to look after them as best I can, and I refuse to have them killed uselessly because of this crazy order." By this time I was completely worked up. "What is more, Pearce," I said, "if you had any guts, it might have occurred to you that No. 9 is part of C Company, which you command and for which you are responsible, just as I am for No. 9, in which case you might have refused to transmit the order to me. However, I am sure my court martial will be an interesting affair." I added casually, "Of course, I am quite prepared to do the job any time after 10.30 p.m." Pearce went off to see the colonel, and I sat down glumly to await the officer's extort, which, no doubt, would shortly be arriving to me.

One hour later, Pearce appeared once more: "It's all right," he said, "the C.O. says you can start work at

10.30 p.m." I gasped, and Pearce actually offered me a drink. "What in the world made the C.O. give that order?" I enquired. Pearce looked rather sheepish. "As a matter of fact," he said, "he hadn't noticed that it would still be light at 8 p.m., and wanted to hear how you had been getting on before he went to bed?" I took No. 9 out at 10.30 p.m. as agreed, and carried out the job successfully. There was only one casualty, a man slightly wounded by a stray bullet. By this time I had come to the conclusion that the colonel was completely irresponsible and unfit to command a battalion or anything else. But I was only a very junior subaltern and there was nothing I could do about it.

One winter's night, a deplorable incident occurred for which none but me were to blame. The fact is that I committed the extremely grave military crime of being drunk and incapable while on duty in the front line. On cold winter nights an issue of rum was made to all men in the front line. It was a thick, reddish liquid, very different to the kind obtainable at a wine merchant's and very rich and potent and the finest I have ever tasted. It was brought up in large, round china receptacles better known as S.R.D. jars, and dished out by the officer who happened to be on duty during the small hours of the night. On this occasion I had had tea in the afternoon, and had turned in for a few hours' sleep before coming on duty from 10 p.m. to 2 a.m. At one o'clock, I went round the line with my batman, Private Archer, handing out the rum. When I had finished, I gave Archer his tot, and finally had one myself. A few minutes later as I was talking to a sentry, I suddenly felt extremely ill. I was violently sick and must have passed out, for, when I came to, I found myself lying in my dugout, with Archer hovering anxiously over me. He had behaved superbly as far as I was concerned. Although even then I was far from being a light-weight, he had carried me down to the dugout, and then returned to clear up the trench. By this time it was 2 a.m., so he went to the officer who was to relieve me, and blandly announced that I had just turned in as I was feeling a little off-colour. Moreover, he must have sworn to secrecy the sentries who had seen what happened. My lapse never leaked out, and neither Archer nor anyone else ever referred to it again. I have a very hard head for alcohol, and, as far as I know, my tot of rum was of the normal quantity that I had given to the men. Probably my condition was due to the fact that I had eaten nothing for nine hours, but that is no excuse for my behaviour, for which I have never ceased to be ashamed.

About 18 months later I had a very unpleasant reminder of what my fate might have been, had it not been for Archer's care of me. I was called to sit on a court martial, the court consisting of a regular colonel, a regular major and myself. The prisoner, a private with an excellent army record, was accused of sleeping at his post while on sentry duty in the front line. The case was extremely simple: the man had received his rum ration just as he started his turn on sentry duty. Half-an-hour later an officer had discovered him fast asleep and not unnaturally smelling of rum. We retired to consider our verdict and, to my horror, I found that my two colleagues proposed to find the man guilty then and there, and sentence him to five years' imprisonment. Remembering my previous experience, although I lacked the pluck to tell them about it, I did what I could to save the man. I said that I considered him not guilty; if the army issued a rum ration that had the effect of sending a good soldier to sleep, then the responsibility was the army's. The other two disagreed with me, and by a majority verdict found the man guilty. I did at least succeed in getting his sentence reduced to two years.

Life was very pleasant in the villages of Buire, Heilly and Dernancourt when out of the trenches. Our arrival, for the first time, at Buire was epic. We had marched down from the line. The weather was wet and C Company was extremely bedraggled. A guide indicated the billet, a comfortable-looking farmhouse with the usual barns round it. Captain Pearce halted the company and knocked on the front door. It was opened by an apprehensive old lady. She gazed at poor Pearce, never a handsome figure at the best of times, and then at the men. "Ah, les Prussians, les Prussians!" she shrieked and bolted into the house amid roars of laughter from the men. She turned out to be slightly, but not objectionably, crazy. She used to follow us timidly round the house, presumably in expectation of being molested by "les Prussians". Eventually, she found out that I could speak French and we got along well enough.

There were other distractions to be found. There was the superb tea shop, in an old chateau in Heilly, kept by two pretty and charming sisters. There were trips, by lorry jumping, to Amiens with dinner at Godbert, one of the finest restaurants in all France. There was also the Divisional Cinema, one of the first started in the British army. It was good value for money. For the sum of three centimes, which included transport by lorry to the cinema, one could enjoy a full programme of films, with two or three extra turns thrown in for good measure, provided by artists of the very first rank. Among them was Basil Hallam[1] the famous creator of *Gilbert the Filbert*. The latter was in a Captive Balloon Section, the unit's name referring to observation balloons tethered to the ground by cables, stationed at Buire and I got to know him quite well. When war broke out, he was starring with Elsie Janis, in the *Passing Show* at the Palace Theatre. When he did not join the army immediately he was shamefully treated by the great British public. Smearing little articles appeared about him in the press, and he was the recipient of numerous white feathers from ill-bred viragoes who considered it their patriotic duty to insult in this way any young men who happened to be wearing civilian clothes. Lady Astor was particularly zealous in this activity.

What they did not know was that the unfortunate Basil Hallam, the best tap dancer of his day, suffered from a malformation of the feet, which had caused him to be rejected no less than three times when he applied to enlist. To improve this condition he used to take long runs round the Inner Circle of Regent's Park every morning and finally succeeded in being accepted for service in the Captive Balloon Section, where marching was not a necessary accomplishment. These captive balloons were freely used by both sides for artillery spotting. The spotters would sit in the nacelle of the balloon, which was then allowed to rise into the

---

[1]   Captain Basil Hallam Radford, No. 1 Army Kite Balloon Section, Royal Flying Corps. Killed in action 20 August 1916. Buried at Couin British Cemetery.

air, attached to a lorry by a cable from a steel winch. These balloons were extremely vulnerable to attack by aeroplane, and when this occurred, the spotter floated down to earth with the aid of a parachute. Poor Basil Hallam was killed during one of these attacks soon after we left the Buire area. When he jumped, his parachute did not open.

Basil Hallam in the few years before the outbreak of the 1914 war was easily the most popular young actor on the English stage. He was an extremely handsome young man, tall, fair, blue-eyed, immaculately turned out in the parts in which he was the *jeune premier*, of which *Gilbert the Filbert* was the most famous. He was a superb stage dancer. As a singer he was not out of the ordinary, although his articulation was excellent. Although he seldom raised his voice, every word came over clearly. Whether singing or speaking with a slight, deliberate drawl, his voice had an effect of gaiety and friendliness that was irresistible. To hear him sing his charming little duet with Elsie Janis "You're here and I'm here, so what do we care?" was a pleasure that I have never forgotten. He was just as likeable off the stage, quiet and absolutely modest. He talked simply and directly, looking straight at his listener and his smile was enchanting.

In March 1916, on returning from leave, I found that the 8th East Surreys had left its old stamping ground and was now on the extreme south of the British line, next to the French in the valley of the River Somme. The French troops on our flank were a high-class division. A few weeks before, the Germans had attacked and captured some trenches in the French sector, and this division had been brought up to recapture them, a task that they carried out successfully. We got along very well with them, and the officers' messes exchanged hospitality while the men swapped souvenirs.

On my arrival I was told that in a couple of days' time, my platoon was to take over duty in the marshes across the causeway. I told Captain Pearce that, with his approval, I would look over the post next morning so as to get the lie of the land, and he at once agreed to the suggestion. Accordingly, I crossed the causeway next morning, looked round the strong point, and went on about 150 yards in front of it to examine the field of fire in the event of an enemy raid. It was a beautiful morning, and the atmosphere was completely peaceful. Suddenly I heard a shout from the strong point, and turned round to find the colonel frantically gesticulating. I went back and found him among about fifty men of another company, on a digging party at the strong point. The colonel excelled himself. He started by cussing me for "giving away the position," although the Germans were almost a mile away and there was marsh reeds and brushwood between us. He then ranted away about my slackness and lack of discipline, with all the discourtesy of which he was a master. It seemed to me wisest to say nothing in front of the men, so, when he had finished, I merely saluted and returned to company headquarters.

Next morning I was surprised to see the colonel approaching, this time all smiles and charm. He said he wanted to have a word with me, and, with his hand on my shoulder, we strolled into the wood together. "I suppose you realise," he said, "that I didn't mean a word of what I said yesterday. I didn't know then what

I know now, that you had full permission from your company commander to be out there." I suddenly felt that I had had enough.

"It is good of you to say so, Sir," I said. "But it would have been even better if those men who were listening yesterday, could be listening to what you are saying now. Your remarks yesterday didn't matter in the least to me personally, I had heard most of them before, but you know perfectly well that by now the story will be all round the battalion. How can I possibly be expected to maintain discipline among the men to whom you have proclaimed what you really think of me? The situation is quite impossible, and the only way out is for me to transfer to another unit. Will you please arrange this?" The colonel seemed surprised and protested half-heartedly, but he was clearly not displeased at this turn of events. A fortnight later, I found that I had been attached to the 55th Trench Mortar Battery. I said good bye to the men of No. 9 platoon and they seemed nearly as regretful as I was. They all shook hands with me, said how sorry they were, wished me luck and told me not to forget them. Then, with my faithful batman, Private Archer, I went off to report to my new unit, more depressed than I had ever been in my life.

I found the battery in billets in the village of Bray, busily preparing to play their part in the great battle, which became known as the First Day of the Somme. Everyone, including the Germans, knew it would soon begin. On a nearby slope a replica of that part of the German line that the brigade was to attack, had been laid out, complete with the names of all the trenches. Rehearsals of the coming operations were carried out, which included the exact timing of artillery barrages and infantry advances. It was a new and admirable idea, for, when the time came, everyone knew exactly what he had to do and where to go.

To explain the importance in the scheme of things of the Stokes mortar, which was a type portable firepower available to infantry, a few words are needed to describe the gun itself. It consisted of several parts: the barrel, bipod and the base plate. One man could carry each part of the gun, unless the ground was impassable to infantry. The gun was muzzle-loading, and the shell three-inches in diameter and 12 pounds in weight. Although it could not destroy field fortifications, its effect on enemy personnel was devastating for its shells exploded with a horrible grinding noise, hurling splinters of steel in all directions. The mortar's rate of fire was so rapid that, when needed, 22 shells could be fired in one minute, with eight of them visible in the air at the same time. The range was, at first, from 190–430 yards. The only disadvantage of the gun was that its fire was not always accurate; the speed of flight of the shells was so relatively slow that they could be deflected by the wind.

The Stokes mortar acted as a sort of supporting artillery to infantry. If properly handled, it could be brought up to support the infantry in battle with a delay of an hour or less, whether the fight was a big one or a local trench raid. It was equally valuable in defence because it could come into action where it was needed far quicker than the fire support usually provided by field artillery. Finally, the gun could be manufactured easily, quickly and cheaply at a cost of only about £40. So, its loss (in battle) was no great matter.

V

First Day Of the Somme

1 July 1916

The battle of the Somme was the most dreadful ordeal ever undergone by the British Army, but I have never succeeded in understanding why it was fought at all, and why such fantastically stupid methods were employed by the Higher Command.

The decision to stage this battle belonged to Marshal Joseph Joffre and General Sir Douglas Haig, who were respectively Commander-in-Chiefs of the French and British armies. The line of attack ran from north of the River Ancre to a point about seven miles south of the River Somme. Joffre and Haig carefully selected for their assault the most strongly defended part of the whole of the German line in France. After the 1914 battles the Germans had deliberately adopted a defensive strategy on the Western Front. Having decided on defence, the Germans made the most of their opportunities.

On the Somme front, the German positions had been very carefully sited in front of the slight range of hills known as the Pozières ridge so that they could overlook our trenches, and keep their guns hidden behind the ridge. The ground was ideal for the construction of earthworks, at which the Germans proved to be far more efficient than our men. I saw some dugouts that were two-storeys and connected by ladders, proof against any shell. There was reportedly even a dugout that contained a grand piano. They had planted barbed-wire entanglements all over the ground. In front of the German front-line trench the width of this wire belt amounted to 20 yards or more.

Higher Command had no new ideas whatever to overcome these formidable difficulties. They used more men than ever before. They had an idea that their previous offensives at Festubert and Loos, both in 1915, had failed owing to an insufficiency of artillery, so hundreds more guns were brought up to pound the German line by day and by night for a week beforehand. At the moment of assault all these guns lifted their ranges, according to carefully-timed programme, so as to keep well in front of the various objectives of the infantry attack. The result was that the Germans, with the exception of a few look-out men, kept their troops in their shell-proof dugouts until our assault began. They then emerged from their dugouts and proceeded to mow down our men with their machineguns, unmolested by our artillery which was firing over their heads. To add to the inaptitude of the Higher Command, no attempt was made to maintain secrecy, so that not only the whole of England, but also the whole German army knew exactly where and when the assault was to take place.

A young artillery officer who took part in the initial assault wrote a brilliant account of it to his parents. In one passage he described how he was sitting in the 8th East Surreys' headquarters an hour before Zero at 7.30 a.m. when Captains Wilfred 'Billie' Nevill and Charles Pearce, commanders of the battalion's B and C companies respectively, entered the dugout. "They were both radiant," he wrote. After the Somme battle, it was seldom, indeed, that we saw any officers or men looking radiant just before going "over the top." Both Pearce and Neville were killed at the very start of the assault.

Billie Nevill[1] certainly deserves a place in this narrative if only because an unimportant incident, for which he was responsible, achieved world fame. He had joined the 8th East Surreys immediately on leaving Dover College. He was an altogether exceptional boy. One of the most popular characters in the battalion, he had an uproarious sense of humour all his own, and he was forever thinking up new ideas. Among other things he produced a *Trench Magazine* entirely written by him. It was somewhat bawdy, full of local 'jokes' and the men loved it. Before the Somme battle began, Nevill had realised the importance of getting his company across no-man's-land with the utmost speed. He therefore presented a football to each of the four platoons,[2] promising a prize to the one whose football arrived first in the German trenches. That was all he had in mind, but some press man got to hear of it and a terrific fuss was made about it both in the British press and in the newspapers of many countries whose sympathies lay with us. The result was that telegrams of congratulations kept arriving at the regimental depot from football clubs as far away as Argentina and long after Nevill had been killed.

---

1 Captain Wilfred 'Billie' Nevill, 8th East Surreys. Killed in action 1 July 1916. Buried at Carnoy Military Cemetery.

2 Nevill provided only two footballs to kick across no-man's-land, not four as is often stated.

The 18th (Eastern) Division returned to the trenches on 23 June 1916 in the sector to the right of its old position in front of Fricourt. On our right was the 30th Division, with its flank on Maricourt. The 18th and 30th were leading XIII Corps' attack at the southern end of Fourth Army's battlefront. Further to the right were the French. The 55th Brigade's front line was about 250–300 yards from the enemy's, facing part of the village of Montauban and its final objective was the German line a few hundred yards on the other side of the Mametz–Montauban ridge. The enemy lines were held by a crack German regiment.

The 55th Trench Mortar Battery was kept very busy preparing for the assault. Gun positions were dug in the front line, hundreds of mortar shells were brought up to Happy Valley, where we inserted the fuses and detonators and then carried them to the front-line position. There was a huge mass of artillery of all calibres sited in and behind Happy Valley, including some extraordinary howitzers belonging to and manned by the French. These antediluvian monsters were said to have been used at the Battle of Sedan, in 1870. Each howitzer was mounted on an enormous wooden platform, and well to the front of it. Each was fired by a long lanyard, and the howitzer, owing to the tremendous force of the recoil, travelled backwards to the rear of the platform, and was then pushed into firing position again by the crew. From the rear of the firing position the whole of the flight of the shell could easily be followed with the naked eye.

On 24 June, the tremendous bombardment of the German positions began and continued with varying intensity until the battle began on 1 July. Our trench mortars took no part in this. My own orders were very simple: at eight minutes before Zero hour at 7.30 a.m. my two Stokes mortars were to open as rapid fire as possible on a small sector of the German front line. At Zero we were to cease fire, and I was to report for orders to the O.C. 8th East Surreys. The attack was originally fixed for 29 June, but was delayed for two days owing to bad weather.

In a battle of this magnitude, divisional commanders had little scope for original tactics, because at the tactical-level the artillery programme was controlled by the various army corps, and this, in turn, controlled the movements of the infantry. Thus, at Zero, the artillery was supposed to lift its shellfire off the German front line and move it to the German support line further back, on which it continued to fire for a stipulated period while the just-captured enemy positions were consolidated. Then there was another artillery lift and the infantry were to continue their advance to the German support lines, and so on. All these periods and barrages were laid down in accordance with the varying distances to be covered, and the times considered necessary to capture the strong points by the infantry. Once the artillery programme had begun, it was extremely difficult, if not impossible, to alter it.

In spite of the rigidity of all this planning, our divisional commander, Major-General Sir Ivor Maxse, took certain steps that showed his quality, and which must have had a very important effect on the result of the battle, as far as the 18th (Eastern) Division was concerned. At several points on the divisional front he ordered narrow tunnels – better known as Russian Saps – to be mined, these only nine feet below the surface. At the far end of these saps, which lay almost underneath the far side of the German barbed wire, a charge was laid that was to be detonated only two minutes before Zero. Thus, if the work had been properly done, as was indeed the case, several new trenches of a sort, running right across no-man's-land, would suddenly come into being. These allowed infantry units subsequently moving forward comparatively safe passage across no-man's-land. Maxse saw that a large rum ration was issued just before the assault, and the day after he doubled the food rations carried up to the front line, together with cigarettes and other small luxuries.

The night of 30 June was comparatively quiet. I was in a dugout with five other subalterns, some from the 55th Trench Mortar Battery and others from the 8th East Surreys, all friends of mine. No one got, or tried to get much sleep, but there was no sign of nervousness or apprehension. We just talked, quietly and happily, through the night. The only strange feature was provided by a boy – to whom, as far as we knew, religion meant nothing – who produced a sheet of paper on which was written, in a sort of mediaeval French, an unusual form of prayer. It had been given to him by the lady at his billet, who told him that those who read it before battle would be protected from death. The boy suggested that we might like to take advantage of this, so I scribbled a translation into English, which was read aloud in turn, by everyone in the dugout, without the slightest self-consciousness. It simply seemed the natural thing to do. Unfortunately, the prayer did not grant total immunity for, next day, out of the six of us in the dugout, one was dead and two seriously wounded.

The first day of July was a glorious sunny day. Hot breakfasts arrived soon after dawn and the men cleaned up and shaved. All positions were taken up. Then, at 6.30 a.m., the bombardment intensified. The din was deafening, almost unimaginable in its intensity and I began to wonder how much more of it I could stand without bursting my eardrums or going crazy. The Germans replied with everything they had, and shells were bursting all over our trenches.

I and my men were sheltering in a dugout near the Stokes guns. At 7.15 a.m., we manned them and seven minutes later, opened fire for all we were worth. The loaders were stripped to the waist and even stood by with cans of water to cool the guns, which would otherwise have become too hot to fire. We found afterwards that my two guns had fired 320 shells altogether in eight minutes. Amid the pandemonium at 7.30 a.m., we ceased fire and saw the division's infantry scrambling out of the front line trench to go "over the top" for the first time.

Looking over the parapet, I saw a most amazing sight. As far as the eye could see on either side, row after row after row of our men were moving steadily forward towards the German trenches. Shells were bursting all over no-man's-land and the air was thick with bullets from machine guns, which seemed to be firing from all directions. Here, a single soldier would fall, there, a whole group would be mown down by a machine gun, or disintegrate when a shell burst among them. But, the lines still moved steadily forward. To me it seemed that these brave men were marching straight to victory, and I was tremendously elated. I could not know that they formed only one seventh of the total British force that had made the assault that day, and, that the other divisions beyond my view had failed in their endeavour and had suffered appalling casualties.

The German fire was at its peak and shells were bursting in the trenches all round me, while I somehow made my way to the 8th East Surreys' headquarters, most of it by crawling on my stomach. Lieutenant-Colonel Alfred Irwin, now in command, was at his best: cheerful, confident and clear headed. He told me to await orders, so I sat down watching the stream of orderlies and runners arriving with their messages, wondering what was going on outside. Three quarters of an hour went by before Irwin called me over. "I don't know the position yet myself," he said. "All I do know is that we are in the Hun front line. You can go over now; get in touch with the battalion, and help them all you can. Good luck, P.G., I shall be coming over myself very soon." He smiled, we shook hands, and I returned to my guns. The previous night, 30 infantrymen had reported to me to carry ammunition. I saw that they were ready and told the corporal in charge to bring his men along some distance behind my own men.

I scrambled out of the trench. The first thing I saw was the body of Captain Pearce, my former company commander in the 8th East Surreys, lying a few yards away, but there was no time to stop to bury him.[1] I made a dart for the opening of the newly blown Russian

---

1   Captain Charles Pearce, 8th East Surreys. Killed in action 1 July 1916. Buried at Carnoy Military Cemetery.

sap 100 yards away. I had got half way when a German machine gun began to traverse, and I leapt for cover into a shell hole, which I found to contain another occupant, one of the East Surreys' men, who had had the same idea as me. We were crouching, actually touching one another, when he suddenly fell against me, dead. A bullet had gone straight through his head. Had he not been there, I should certainly have been hit.

I looked round and saw my gun teams, eight men in all, nearby. Taking advantage of a lull in the machine-gun fire, I bolted for the Russian sap and dived in head first. The gun teams followed and we made our way unmolested along the sap, which had blown a hole in the German barbed-wire belt and ended only a few yards from their front-line trench, into which we jumped. Its sole inhabitants at this point were three dead, extremely dead, Germans, with two or three other corpses round the traverse on each side. The bottom of the trench was littered with strips of what I at once recognised to be Stokes mortar shells. This was the exact spot that had been our target for the eight minutes before Zero, and I felt very glad that the first part of our job had been carried out properly and that we had been able to be of some help to the 8th East Surreys in their assault.

Then I made an unwelcome discovery. While all of my men had followed me and, with the exception of one slightly wounded case, were there in the trench with me, not one of the shell carriers had followed their example. So, having had the luck to arrive safely in the German line, here we were, quite impotent for lack of ammunition. There was only one thing to be done. I told the men to stay where they were and, accompanied by my sergeant, made the return rush to our old front line, where I found the carriers sheltering in their dugout.

I was furious with them. Owing to their failure to do their job, my gunners were sitting uselessly in the captured German front line, when they should have been up supporting the infantry attack. Also, thanks to them, I had already crossed no-man's-land twice with the prospect of having to do it yet again. Luckily I managed to restrain myself, and soon realised that they were by no means solely to blame. Carrying Stokes-mortar shells in battle was a horrible job. Each man was supposed to carry six shells; three on his chest and three on his back in a sort of waist-coat with compartments to contain the shells. Thus, in addition to ordinary equipment, these soldiers had to lug 72 pounds of dead weight of steel across no-man's-land, and, if all went well, for another one-and-a-quarter miles. As if this were not enough, should a bullet strike one of the shells, the result for him would be certain and dreadful death. If the fuse of a mortar shell caught alight, it would burn for nine seconds, far too short a time to enable him to get rid of the shell, and he would then inevitably be blown to pieces. Good soldiers could, and would, undertake this work under trusted leadership, but, as I only then found out, these men had no leadership at all. The battalion commander had simply ordered each of his companies to detail so many men to make up the number. There they were, a confused mob under the leadership of a singularly inefficient corporal who was unknown to most of them.

I realised that I should get nowhere if I tried to drive them, so I tried a little persuasion. I explained how vital it was for the shells to be carried across to help the infantry advance. I pointed out that German fire in no-man's-land was lessening, and I explained that, once they reached the sap, the rest of the journey was easy. I also reduced the load for each man from six to five shells. Then we started out once more, I in the lead and my sergeant bringing up the rear. It was by no means an easy passage, although the enemy fire was certainly less than before. On reaching the sap, I found that the situation was not too bad. Two of the carriers had been wounded, and some had disappeared again. We now had 100 shells ready to be used. This was a sufficient number for immediate purposes, but we were already behind the timetable, so I decided to go on. We picked up the Stokes-mortar teams and made our way at snail's pace through the labyrinth of German trenches. We met with no trouble on the way, and the only people we saw were wounded carried on stretchers, and a few parties of prisoners. We entered a corner of Montauban village at about 1 p.m., and continued up the ridge. There, a few hundred yards down the opposite slope, was our final objective, and it was full of 8th East Surreys' men.

We made our way down and were greeted with enthusiasm, and found ourselves at once involved in the only comic incident of that tragic day. About 300 yards beyond the trench we could see what was obviously a German field-gun emplacement. The infantry company commander wished to send out a party to reconnoitre it, and I suggested that if any Germans were still in occupation a few rounds of fire from my guns would soon bring them out. I fired one round. In a few seconds, a white handkerchief was hoisted, tied to the end of a rifle. I ceased fire. A *pickelhaube* [German leather helmet with a decorative spike on top], then made its appearance, but, to our astonishment, its wearer who climbed out of the trench was seen to be wearing khaki. He then cheered at the top of his voice, and after executing an extempore war dance, ran briskly over to us amid roars of laughter from the men. He turned out to be a comic character from an adjoining company, who had been doing a little reconnaissance on his own – for souvenirs – without waiting for orders. The only other occupants of the emplacement were some dead German gunners. The gun itself was still there and was dragged back later on by one of our artillery gun teams.

The 8th East Surreys' men were in a tremendous state of elation. In their first big fight they had arrived at their final objective at 12.30 p.m., after giving a thrashing to one of the best regiments in the German army. Among the 8th East Surreys' subalterns was an immensely powerful individual, South African by birth, named Janion. After getting into the German front line he had gone completely berserk. Armed with a rifle and bayonet he was seen to kill 10 Germans, most of them with the latter weapon, for which he was awarded the D.S.O. He always maintained that he knew nothing whatever about his actions on 1 July, for, after consuming a man's-sized ration of rum, he remembered no more until he found himself in the German line.

It was grand to see the high spirits of the men. They were wandering about, many wearing a German *pickelhaube*, smoking huge German cigars, shaking hands with their officers, and swapping yarns about their adventures in the fighting. They had followed their young platoon commanders through hell, and would have gladly done it all over again. In fact, the battalion commanders sent back word to 55th Brigade headquarters indicating their position and asking permission to continue the advance. An hour later came the anti-climax to the unutterable disappointment of us all. Orders arrived that we were to stay where we were and consolidate the position.

All who had taken part in the fighting were furious at the way in which their efforts had been wasted by the Higher Command, and their resentment was more than justified. I myself saw strings of German lorries disappearing in the far distance towards the east, in the evening of 1 July. Two days later, Lieutenant-Colonel Francis Maxwell V.C.[1] of the 12th (Service) Battalion, The Duke of Cambridge's Own (Middlesex Regiment), in the 54th Brigade, reconnoitred two miles beyond the new front line without encountering any Germans. In previous assaults at the Battles of Loos and Festubert the initial success had been wasted because the reserve had been left so far back, that they arrived too late to exploit it. Here the reserves were well up on the spot. We saw them for ourselves, cavalry and infantry, bivouacking in the Happy Valley. It never seems to have occurred to the Higher Command, as it did to us, that, even a comparatively small, determined, fast moving force pushed through the 15-kilometre-wide gap and advancing north east towards the River Ancre, while the Germans were off their balance, could capture their

---

1   Brigadier-General Francis Maxwell V.C. Killed in action 21 September 1917. Buried at Ypres Reservoir Cemetery.

artillery in the Ancre valley and, attacking from their rear, might well surround them and destroy them.

On 1 July, the 18th (Eastern) Division had suffered 3,707 casualties. This included 45 officers and 871 other ranks killed, plus 103 officers and 2692 other ranks wounded. Each battalion in the division could be described as a band of brothers. In the 8th East Surreys there were four pairs of brothers among the officers, and many more among the men. For two years they had lived, played, worked and trained together. Close friendships and deep affections had been created, so that, to me, and indeed to all the survivors of that battle, the sense of personal loss was almost unbearable. Half the 8th East Surreys' officers were casualties, with three of the four company commanders killed. There was hardly anything left of my grand No. 9. Platoon. Nine of the men had been killed before the battle by one of our own heavy trench-mortar shells (from an artillery unit in no way connected with my Stokes battery) that fell short. The rest of the platoon was in the first wave of the attack, and there were very few survivors. My splendid little platoon sergeant, Howard, had a terrible shell wound in the back. Happily, he survived, although crippled. For many years ran an excellent pub in his native Ipswich.

The losses suffered by the 55th Brigade on 1 July were very heavy. The full strength of one battalion was rather more than 1000 men. After the battle, the 7th Queens had but 380 men left, and the 8th East Surreys only a few more. The 7th West Kents, who had been the reserve battalion in the battle, were, however, still more or less up to strength. On 13 July, the 7th West

Kents were thrown into the fight for the capture of Trônes Wood, a bloody and confused affair in which men stalked each other by night among the tree stumps, while the whole wood was pounded indiscriminately by German and British artillery. The remainder of the brigade took no part in this beyond providing fatigue and ration parties.

On relief, after a few days' rest, the brigade was moved to a quieter sector of the British line, Bois-Grenier near Armentières. It returned to the Somme battlefield in mid-September.

Two new officers reported for duty with the battery. The first was Captain K.M. McIver, who took over command. Up to then, the question of command had never been properly settled. Two lieutenants, both easy going individuals, had been the senior officers, and, in practice, matters had been left to settle themselves. McIver came from the Orkney Islands. If he was typical of their inhabitants, they must be a singularly dour people. He was 40 years of age, which was old for this kind of work, strict, quite humourless and almost fanatically patriotic. But he was a good and brave officer. He and I got on well. The other newcomer, Lieutenant Henry Conybeare, a Canadian, was one of the very worst officers I met: a lanky, ginger-haired individual perpetually talking in a nasal whine, grumbling, running down England, and boasting, although he had never been in action. However, there he was and we had to put up with him.

VI

Schwaben Redoubt

September 1916

On 25 September 1916 we went into the line once more, in front of Thiepval on the Somme. The village of Thiepval was situated near the River Ancre. Behind it, the ground sloped gently up to the Pozières ridge, and here the Germans had constructed two huge redoubts, Stuff Redoubt and Schwaben Redoubt. The 36th (Ulster) Division had attacked the position on 1 July and had succeeded in capturing part of the Schwaben, but had been driven out again after suffering fearful casualties. The position had now become of the utmost importance to the Germans.[1] Since 1 July, attack after attack, at Fricourt, Guillemont, Pozières and Flers, had placed most of the Pozières ridge in our possession. Thus, the eventual loss of Thiepval and the Schwaben would mean that the German artillery positions in the Ancre valley would be overlooked and become untenable, so that the whole German line would have to be withdrawn.

For two years the position had been held by various German regiments, including the crack Infantry

---

1   Schwaben Redoubt was regarded by the German army as a key position in its defences astride the River Ancre, and more generally north of the River Somme.

Regiment 180 from Württemberg. Nothing was left of the village but for a piece of the church tower and a few stones. Over the rest of the ground the Germans had built an immense labyrinth of trenches, ammunition dumps, two-storey-deep dugouts, machine-gun emplacements, and barbed-wire entanglements 20 yards wide. Everything possible had been done to render this place impregnable to a British attack.

The attack on Thiepval and Schwaben Redoubt, 26–30 September 1916 was made by the 53rd and 54th Brigades who captured the village, and part of the Schwaben and held on to their gains. It was a wonderful feat of arms. Major-General Sir Ivor Maxse, who commanded 18th (Eastern) Division, made brilliant use of his artillery. Instead of using the futile system of "lifts," he employed the "rolling barrage," which is better known as a "creeping barrage". This meant that, at the moment of attack, the artillery laid down a "curtain" of shellfire in no-man's-land behind which the infantry assembled. The artillery then increased its ranges, little by little, to destroy and suppress German defences and infantry. The infantry advanced close behind the curtain of fire. To achieve success, absolute accuracy on the part of the artillery was vital, together with considerable courage on the part of the infantry in keeping close up. A good deal of practice in this was carried out beforehand. The 55th Brigade relieved the remnants of the 53rd and 54th Brigades in the Schwaben Redoubt. The approach trenches were deep, so that we were able to bring the guns up by daylight. The brigade's job was to hold on to what had been gained, and, if possible, to capture still more of the redoubt, working up the slope.

I and my two Stokes mortars were with the 7th Buffs. On the right flank were the 8th East Surreys and on the left the 7th West Kents. We had only been in position for half an hour when the East Surreys went "over the top". They got into the German trench, but lost so many men, including some of their finest non-commissioned officers and officers, that the survivors were forced back to their starting point.

For the next eight days life in the Schwaben became a grisly, chaotic nightmare. It formed a theme worthy of the pen of Dante, or the brush of Goya. It is impossible to give an exact and coherent account of what went on; soldiers of two armies, using the deadliest weapons hitherto invented, were fighting with the utmost fury. Meanwhile, the disputed ground was being pounded continuously and apparently indiscriminately with shellfire by the artillery of both sides. The Germans had the advantage of knowing the ground far better than we did. At numerous parts of the redoubt bomb-stops[1] had been erected, and these were continually changing hands, usually to our advantage. When the 55th Brigade was eventually relieved it held the whole of the Schwaben Redoubt, except for one corner. Most of these small attacks were organised on the spot by subalterns. The usual procedure was for the men on our side of the bomb-stop to hurl a steady shower of Mills bombs on to the Germans on the other side. While this was going on, another section of our men would crawl out of the trench and then take a running leap on to

---

[1] A bomb-stop is either a barricade or a traverse in a trench to stop either the blast or shrapnel, or both, of an explosion travelling any distance along its length, or the progress of enemy attackers.

the German defenders busily engaged in hurling bombs at the "*Englander*" on the other side of the bomb-stop.

At about 6.30 a.m., I was drinking a cup of tea with some 7th Buffs' officers when a sergeant from the 7th West Kents entered the dugout. We were glad to see him, for, although we knew that the 7th West Kents were on our left, we had not, up to then, been able to establish proper contact with them. The sergeant, an elderly man, was given some tea, but sat on with us showing no sign of wishing to return to his unit. Most likely the prospect of doing the return journey alone did not appeal to him. Finally, and probably tactlessly, I suggested that he should clear off and leave us room to move in the dugout. He looked hard at me, and said: "Will you come with me, Sir? If you do, my officer and you will be able to draw up the exact position on the map." I agreed, and away we went, floundering through the waterlogged trenches. The sergeant still seemed uneasy. After 10 minutes or so he said: "It's not too far now, Sir. If you care to wait here, I'll go to get my officer." He continued on his way, and I stayed where I was, peering over the top of the trench to examine my position.

It was a foggy, rainy morning, and, apart from the interminable labyrinth of trenches running in all directions, the only object of interest was a large mound about 60 or 70 yards away, looming up above the trench line, and apparently formed by a huge heap of sand bags. I could see no sign of any movement, so I placidly sat down to await the return of the old sergeant. Some minutes later, back he came, accompanied by a young 7th West Kents' subaltern, Lieutenant Douglas Sutherst by name, who afterwards joined our battery, and turned out to be a fine officer. He seemed considerably startled to find me sitting there.

"Good God," Sutherst said. "Do you know where you are?"

"No," I replied, "except that your sergeant brought me here, I have no idea."

"Do you see that thing?" he said, pointing to the mound.

"Of course I can," I snapped. "I'm not blind. What about it?"

"The Germans are on the other side," he said.

Entirely without thinking, I said: "Why not get them out of it?"

Sutherst looked at me as if I was mad and, indeed, the idea that two subalterns and a sergeant, armed only with revolvers, could capture the mound must have sounded ridiculous.

I had had an idea. The normal minimum range of a Stokes gun was 190 yards. From where I was the mound was much too close to be a target. But, we had recently received a couple of experimental new guns in which a hole had been drilled at the bottom of the barrel, so that when the cartridge in the bottom of the shell hit the stud at the back of the gun which fired it, much of the gas generated would escape through the hole, and the shell would only travel for a greatly reduced distance. The size of the hole could be reduced by moving a small lever, which, in turn, moved a flange to cover the hole, as required. It was a somewhat amateur gadget. At the time little was known as to its effect on the range of the gun, and there had been accidents caused by shells detonating and bursting without leaving the barrel at all. In point of fact, this feature was discarded soon afterwards. I had suddenly remembered that one of my guns was fitted with this gadget.

"Listen," I said to Sutherst, "I am a Stokes gunner. I am going back to get a gun. If we let off a few rounds from here, we shall find out fast enough if there are any Huns there."

I got back to my guns, and came back again accompanied by one gun team of three men, my sergeant, and two men carrying 10 shells. Aiming the gun carefully, I opened up the hole at the bottom of the gun to its full extent, and, hoping for the best, fired one round. The shell left the gun all right, and sailed over the mound. We heard the burst but nothing happened. The second shell was fired with the same result. Altering the direction of the gun very slightly, I fired a third shell, which duly left the gun following the same course as its predecessors. Nine seconds later there was a terrific explosion and the mound seemed to be disintegrating. Then I saw a human body hurled 20 or 30 feet into the air and fall again. To my horror, it appeared to be wearing a khaki uniform. Amid the general confusion and fighting going on all over the Schwaben, Sutherst might easily have been mistaken, and I must have been shooting at a post held by our own infantry. I at once ordered the team to stop firing.

Suddenly, through the mist, I saw a white flag appear and the man carrying it, obviously a German soldier (thank God!) climbed slowly out of the trench and stood there uncertainly. We waved to him, and after some hesitation, he began to make his way towards us.

Then, to my amazement, he was followed by another, and another, and another. Thirty-two German soldiers came stumbling over to surrender. Something very odd must have happened to them, for, although none of them were wounded, all were shaking uncontrollably, and some seemed to be gibbering.

I decided to interrogate the prisoners to find out the situation in the mound, and saw no reason why I should not try to do so. The language presented no problem. In 1912, I spent six months studying German and spoke it well. Questioning prisoners could be a tricky affair owing to the Hague Convention, which laid down that the only information that a prisoner was going to give was his name, rank and regimental number. If the interrogating officer was clumsy or the prisoner recalcitrant, the latter merely had to keep quiet. In theory, nothing would happen to him. I had heard of the bullying methods supposedly used by the Germans to obtain instant obedience, but I was useless at this kind of thing. I talked to the prisoners in a friendly way, as if I was talking to my own men. "*Kinder*," I began. "*Kinder*" is a very friendly German word. Besides meaning "children," it can be used by a host at a party to his guests, or by the popular foreman of a gang to his mates. It was the right approach. The prisoners looked at me with interest, and some were smiling.

Any prisoner of war has good reason to be apprehensive, at least during the first hour or two of captivity. In every army there are trigger-happy soldiers and badly trained men who will shoot at anyone wearing enemy uniform, whatever the circumstances. In every army there are a very few sadistic soldiers who, ostensibly to avenge some comrade, will shoot prisoners in cold blood, if they think they can get away with it by reporting them shot while escaping. There are even whole units with an evil reputation for not taking prisoners.

So, these German soldiers must have been relieved to find themselves addressed by a young officer, in their own language, who treated them as human beings. "Now, boys," I said, speaking in German, "the war is over for you. You are going down the line and will be well treated. Before you go, I want to know if any of your mates are still alive over there, and what your defences are like." One man replied: "*Alle todt, alles kaputt, Herr Leutnant.*" (Everyone's dead, everything's broken, Lieutenant) Others began to join in, but I stopped them and sent them down the line under escort.

I had learned what I wanted to know, and the Schwaben Redoubt was no place for what the Germans call a "*Kaffeeklatsch*" (coffee gossip). I turned to Sutherst in excitement. "That man," I said, "told me that they were all dead over there, and that their defences are smashed to bits. I'm sure we can get that trench for nothing if we are quick enough. One of your sections should be enough for the job, and I will bring my men over to keep you company."

Sutherst rushed down the trench and was back in no time with a dozen men. We all made a dash for the mound. As I thought, not a shot was fired at us. I have never seen such a dreadful sight as that trench, which was about 100 yards long. It was crammed with corpses and bits of corpses scattered all over the place. Forty of them were counted afterwards. Then we saw what had created this holocaust. The trench, a very deep one hitherto untouched by artillery, was an enormous ammunition dump for front line troops, and must have served most of the Thiepval defences. Small-arms ammunition, grenades and mortar shells, mostly exploded, were lying about in the widest confusion. Our shell had blown up the whole arsenal. No wonder those Germans were shaking and gibbering.

We explored up the trench to our right and came to a traverse; on the other side of which was a large dugout with two entrances, the kind that the Germans built to accommodate about 100 men. We clearly heard talking down below, and shouted to the inhabitants to come out. The talking stopped abruptly, but no one came out. We shouted again and again without result, so we rolled two Stokes shells down each entrance. Nine seconds later, the shells exploded and smoke and fire came out of the entrances. We had set the dugout on fire and the inmates had come to a speedy end. What we did may sound barbarous. This was because during previous and subsequent British assaults a few Germans would stay in their dugouts until the attack had passed over them. They would then emerge with machine guns, so that the attackers were caught between two fires. In the 18th (Eastern) Division we used a wave of "moppers up," whose job it was to halt in the German front line and "mop up" all dugouts, capturing or killing any enemy who resisted. We had done this on 1 July and thus had been able to take our objectives without interference from the rear. So we "mopped up" this dugout near the mound. It was necessary; we were trained to do it and we did it.

At this point I told Sutherst I would take my gun team back. He led his men further up the trench until they came to a bomb-stop where they were held up. I had good reasons for my decision. Firstly, I had only three rounds of ammunition left. If Sutherst wanted further Stokes mortar support, there were two of our guns with the West Kents. Secondly, strictly speaking, I was not doing my job, which was to support the 7th Buffs in defence, and not the 7th West Kents in attack. Should the 7th Buffs be attacked and I was not there, serious trouble might ensue. Finally, matters were getting out of hand. After all, our handful of men could not be expected to capture the Schwaben on their own. It was time to report on our action so that brigade could take over. We returned, to our starting point and I sent down a report to our battery headquarters. Curiously enough, both army and divisional headquarters knew what had happened long before my report had arrived. Long afterwards, I attended a lecture by a Royal Flying Corps pilot on ground–air communications by wireless. As it turned out, he was flying over Thiepval during our action, had seen the whole thing and had promptly reported it.

We had caught the Germans on the wrong foot. At a cost to ourselves of no casualties and several rounds of Stokes' ammunition, we had put about 100 Germans out of action, of whom we had actually seen 40 corpses and 32 prisoners, not to mention those killed in the dugout. We had captured a key trench, about 200 yards long, in the middle of the Schwaben Redoubt. We had also destroyed a huge ammunition dump. It would take the Germans at least 24 hours to repair the damage in this sector. They would have to send up reinforcements to fill the gap, and replenish the ammunition dump. They would also have to cover their new front with barbed wire, which they could only do at night. They would further have to alter their artillery arrangements and, after what had happened, the morale of their men cannot have been good.

We should have attacked as soon as possible. Two companies, preceded by an artillery barrage, could probably have done the job, and it should not have taken more than five or six hours to arrange this. The attack could have dashed straight across to the far side of the Schwaben, cutting the garrison in two and making it possible to round them up and capture the whole redoubt. The whole of the Pozières ridge would have been in our hands; we should have observation over the River Ancre valley, making untenable the whole of the position of the German artillery sited in it. The Germans would have been forced to retreat, but, where to? A few weeks previously, Field Marshal Paul von Hindenburg and General Erich Ludendorff had taken over command of the German army on the Western Front. Ludendorff's first action was to order the construction of a formidable defence line, from 10–40 miles behind the Somme battlefield, known to us as the Hindenburg line, but also as the Drocourt–Queant line and Siegfried Line. But, in September 1916, construction had hardly begun. If we had had captured the whole of the Schwaben Redoubt, the Germans would have had a serious problem on their hands.

It was not to be, thanks to the inactivity and spinelessness of the brigadier commanding the 55th

Brigade. Brigadier-General Sir Thomas Jackson was ordered again and again by divisional headquarters to attack, and refused to do so. The frontage we had won, about 200 yards, was, he said, too narrow to make an attack practicable. He had lost a lot of men on the previous day owing to the abortive attack of the 8th East Surreys, and this had probably upset him. The man had completely lost his head. Eyewitnesses at brigade headquarters described him as pacing up and down the dugout muttering "My poor men, my poor men." He gave no orders at all to deal with the situation and left it to the front-line troops to make the best of it. When the division was relieved, he was dismissed from his command by Major-General Maxse and sent home. I never spoke to him personally. He was said to be a very pleasant man, but he should never have been allowed to command a brigade.

From then on, life in the Schwaben Redoubt became a hideous nightmare. Ever since, quite seriously, I have felt that hell can hold no terror for anyone who, as I did, spent eight days there. Attacks, at one place or another, seemed to be going on all day long. We would be called to assist the infantry in attacking some enemy strong point; hardly had we finished when we would be called to some other point where the Germans seemed about to break through. It was a real continuous soldiers' battle, for even the battalion commanders were receiving no instructions from brigade. Each subaltern (and if he was killed, his sergeant) had to use his guts, intelligence and initiative to do the best he could in any circumstances and these attributes, together with the bravery of the men, frustrated all that the German Army could do to retake the Schwaben.

It was impossible to shave or wash. Food consisted of nothing but bully beef and biscuits. It began to rain again and this continued for most of the period, making the trenches almost impassable. Even in dry spells it was not easy to get along the main trenches, for the simple reason that corpses in various stages of decomposition lay along them in some places two or even three deep, and they stank to high Heaven.

At one point, one of our guns was in support of a section defending a strong point. Suddenly a party of Germans stormed into the trench, overrunning the infantry. One of our men, Private George Lake of the 7th Buffs,[1] turned to his mates and said quietly: "Get the gun back. I am staying here." He did stay there. Singlehandedly he held up the attack for 10 minutes. Eventually the inevitable happened and he was killed by a bomb, but the Stokes gunners got away safely with their weapon. That was the kind of thing that was going on continuously in the Schwaben and Lake was typical of the brave men of the division who fought there.

Any proper rest at night was out of the question. One night my men and I were in a small dugout, trying to get a little rest during a very heavy artillery bombardment of our trenches when a stretcher party came in, carrying a man who had been blown up by a shell, and who, although only slightly wounded, had

---

1 Private George Lake M.M., 7th Buffs. Killed in action 3 October 1916. Named on Thiepval Memorial.

gone off his head. They asked my permission to leave him in the dugout until it became possible to evacuate him. In the circumstances I had to agree. A little later, four more men, wounded in the bombardment, were brought down. Up to then, the first man had been fairly quiet, but, without warning, he began to rave and yell, making an appalling noise, and kept it up. The other four who, as far as I knew were not shell shock cases, remained quiet for several minutes and then, one by one, began to copy the example of the first man. The racket was exactly like what, I presume, goes on in a padded cell of a lunatic asylum, and I began to feel that if it went on much longer I should begin to join in. My men tried to quieten them, without success. I could not throw them into the trench outside, which was being heavily shelled, and I had not the faintest notion as to how to set about the prevention of what seemed to be becoming a case of collective hysteria. In desperation, I picked up the handle of an entrenching tool and cracked it over the head of the first man with considerable force. I doubt whether this would be considered as the orthodox treatment for such cases, but it had the required effect for it knocked the man unconscious and, when he came to a little later, he gave no more trouble. I suppose my methods of cure did not appeal to the other four wounded, for they, too, stopped their noise.

All troops in the Schwaben were relieved after four days, which was the maximum time that they could reasonably be asked to spend there under such appalling conditions. I had been told Lieutenant Henry Conybeare, the Canadian, would bring up the reserve gun teams to relieve us, so I was surprised when they arrived, two hours late, with Captain K.M. McIver leading them. I was appalled at what he had to tell me. Two days previously Conybeare had gone sick with dysentery. The Medical Officer (M.O.) who was called in, was attached to the battalion in which Conybeare had previously served, and, knowing him of old, refused to certify that he was unfit for duty in the line. So, in spite of his moaning, Conybeare had been forced to start on his way up the line with the gun teams. They had not gone far before a shell burst 300 yards away, whereupon Conybeare had thrown some kind of fit, and had insisted that his servant should help him back to the battery headquarters. On arrival, he had sent the servant to fetch an M.O. from another battalion who had issued a certificate that his patient was suffering from shell shock and was unfit for duty in the trenches. Consequently, at the moment, our Mr. Conybeare was happily sitting in bed drinking whisky, and, as there was no other officer to replace him, I should have to remain in the Schwaben for another four days. It was a grim prospect for me.

For the next three days I carried on in the same frightful conditions as before, clambering over stinking corpses in the mud and trying to help the infantry, repelling bomb attacks, seeing that ammunition and rations were sufficient, in spite of the losses incurred each day by the carrying parties. I was unwashed and unshaved, and never got more than two hours' sleep each night. Most of the time it rained, and the artillery bombardment went on and on.

After the exhilaration of our first day's adventure had worn off, I had found myself, somewhat to my surprise, in a state of blind fury directed at the wooden-headed barbarians over the way, who worshipped war and who, in their attempt to conquer Europe, had forced us to live in a hell from which there was no one way of escape, and to behave like beasts under conditions that no wild beast could tolerate. I kept thinking how splendid it would be if the whole lot of us could be let loose on the Germans with the bayonet to settle the matter once and for all. During the second period, this feeling disappeared. I did not feel particularly frightened, but, although I managed to do what I had to, I felt myself becoming sleepier and more apathetic. When the last day came, I felt that I, for the first time, understood what it meant to be dead-and-alive. I hardly left the dugout and found it extremely difficult to talk at all.

We were relieved by the 28th Division. The officer who was to take my place was a mere boy, but very good looking and alert. I never knew his name, never saw him again, and never heard what became of him, but I shall always remember with gratitude the way in which he behaved that night. Normally, on relief, one had to hand over all stores and ammunition to the relieving officer who checked everything and signed a receipt. When that was done, one had to take him round the gun positions, indicate any special targets and other features, and explain the local situation. This boy came down into the dugout, saw me and promptly produced a large whisky flask, the first I had seen for several days. Then he said: "You look as if you have had too much. I've taken over now. Collect your men and get out of here as quick as you can." I sent an orderly to tell the men to come to the dugout. Then I said to them: "It's no use pretending, I'm done for, and can't do any more. We have just been relieved, but I can't even lead you out of here back to headquarters. Does anyone feel that he can do so?" One of the orderlies, Private Otterway by name, a big, taciturn man, said he thought he could.

"All right Otterway," I said. "You are now in charge of the gun-teams. I will try to keep up in the rear." We set off through that horrible labyrinth stumbling over the corpses, and I brought up the rear, half-carried along by Private Archer. Otterway behaved superbly. It was raining hard and the night was pitch dark, but he never made a mistake and led us through the trenches on which the never-ending bombardment was crashing down. Gradually the shellfire lessened as we got further away from the front line, until we reached a hollow out of range of the German field guns. We stopped here to rest. Somebody said, "Thank God," and quite spontaneously we all shook hands with one another. At last we arrived at battery headquarters. I dismissed the men, but called up Otterway: "You did a fine job," I said. "I don't know how we should have got back alive without you, and I know we are all grateful to you, er, Corporal Otterway." He looked rather startled and said: "Beg pardon, Sir?" "Yes," I replied. "I said 'Corporal Otterway' and meant it. If you could do what you did tonight, you are quite capable of commanding a gun team. Congratulations, Corporal."

After a long sleep, Captain McIver sent me straight off to Le Treport for a fortnight's rest at a new camp just inaugurated by G.H.Q. There were two enclosures of tents, one for officers, and the other for men who, although not wounded or ill, had been exhausted in the Somme battles and needed complete rest. It was a most comfortable place. The food was excellent and there was even a bar. Our party was greeted by a nice old colonel, who told us that there were no rules and we could do exactly what we liked. If anyone wanted to spend a night out of camp (leering at us knowingly), we were welcome to do so, but in that case, perhaps we would be good enough to notify him beforehand (another leer) if possible.

I spent a delightful fortnight in Le Treport and Dieppe, only marred by one slight contretemps, when some of us thumbed a lift back to camp in a resplendent motor car, which turned out to belong to the Commander-in-Chief of the Belgian Army. Unfortunately, when nearly back to camp, we met the old gentleman out for a constitutional on his horse. The car stopped and I explained the situation in my best French. The general was charming and insisted that the car should take us all back to the camp. I'm afraid the chauffeur got a nasty dressing-down when he got home again.

On my return to the 55th Trench Mortar Battery, now quite recovered, I discussed the Conybeare affair with McIver. I said that I thought he should be court-martialed for cowardice at once, but if this could not be done I wanted McIver to know that I would never go into the line again with Conybeare in any capacity. I was sure that McIver would understand my reasons and act accordingly, but, if not, I was prepared to take the consequences. McIver was very sympathetic and sensible. He said that, in any case, he would not allow Conybeare to remain in the battery, but that it might be difficult to arrange the court-martial. The authorities never liked holding officers' courts-martial unless they were very sure of the guilt of the accused, and in this case Conybeare might well get away with it by making use of the M.O.'s certificate. He promised to talk the matter over with the brigadier. Conybeare and I, not unnaturally, were not on speaking terms, but with the others he was as talkative and offensive as before, exactly as if nothing had happened. He seemed to have quite recovered from his indisposition.

The next day McIver, Conybeare and I were summoned to brigade headquarters. The new brigadier – Brigadier-General George "Dicky" Price, who had replaced Jackson – had previously commanded the 7th Bedfords in the 54th Brigade, and was a well-known character in the 18th (Eastern) Division, owing to his command of forceful language, although he was a good-hearted little man and was well liked. In appearance, he was not unlike what Captain Hook might have been like had he lived to middle age. He only had one eye, in which a monocle was invariably fixed, and wore a black patch over the spot where the other one should have been. He had also lost a leg but got about very well with the aid of an artificial leg and there were numerous ribald jokes in circulation as to what happened to this limb when its owner retired for the night. The brigadier invited McIver to explain what Conybeare had, or rather had not, done, and McIver gave a very accurate and sober report, the brigadier, meanwhile, glaring at Conybeare through the monocle.

When McIver had finished, the brigadier asked Conybeare what he had to say. The latter, with the virtuous look of a misjudged man, produced from his pocket the medical certificate. He had hardly begun to speak before the brigadier went into action. "Put that thing away," he roared, "I don't want to see it. You, Mr. Conybeare, are a coward, which is bad, and you have let down a brother officer, which is worse. The 55th Trench Mortar Battery is a fine unit, and you are not fit to belong to it. You will return at once to your battalion, and your name will be placed at the bottom of its leave roster. And, Mr. Conybeare, I am giving instructions to your colonel that, when the battalion goes "over the top" again, you will go with it in the first wave, and that he will take measures to see that you keep up with it. You are a very nasty fellow, and I don't want to see you again. You may go." I never saw Conybeare again. The brigadier's orders were duly carried out, and Conybeare was badly wounded in the next assault made by his battalion.

VII

Regina Trench

November 1916

We returned to the trenches early in November 1916, about a mile away from Thiepval, looking down towards the village of Miraumont in the valley of the River Ancre. We occupied what was known as Regina Trench, and the German position, Desire Trench, was nearly 600 yards away so that our position was not particularly dangerous. In all other respects it was a miserable spot, a quagmire of shell holes, as far as the eye could see, filled by the rain, which poured down day after day. The fatigue parties, bringing up rations and ammunition had a terrible time, and the way the orderlies managed to carry their messages through all the mud in pitch darkness was almost miraculous.

On 18 November we attacked Desire Trench during a snowstorm. Our attack formed part of an assault on a much wider front, on limited objectives. On our right was a Canadian division whose attack was successful. On their left, the 8th East Surreys, to whom my section of Stokes guns of the 55th Trench Mortar Battery was attached, captured Desire Trench without very much difficulty. But, the 19th (Western) Division, on the left of the 18th, lost direction in the mist and went too far to the left. This caused a gap into which the German machine guns penetrated with the result that two companies of the 7th Queens were wiped out. The 7th Buffs were thrown in to close the gap, and neared the objective, but were withdrawn by order next day, as the 19th's troops had retired to their starting point.

My orders were to bring over my guns an hour after Zero. I was waiting to go over, outside the aid post, when Captain Edward 'Gimmie' Gimson, the 8th East Surreys' doctor, called me in. Knowing that I spoke German, he pointed out an elderly prisoner, crouching in a corner, and asked me to try to find out what was the matter with him. I went over to the old German, sat down by him and asked what the trouble was. He turned his head towards me and said very quietly: "*Ich bin blind, ich kann nicht sehen*" (I am blind, I can't see). He leaned over towards me, and died in my arms.

The line of attack of the 8th East Surreys lay down a broad ravine. I got my guns safely to Desire Trench through considerable machine-gun fire and shelling, to find a brisk bombing fight in progress. The Germans were attacking up a communication trench, and I could see the tops of their arms turning over as they threw their bombs, using the same action as a cricket bowler. I fired several rounds, and after a few minutes the Germans became discouraged and gave up the attack, leaving Desire Trench safely in the hands of the East Surreys.

When matters became calmer I noticed that we were standing close to the entrance of a fair-sized dugout, the very place to shelter my gun teams. As we went down to investigate we were met by an appalling stench, which emanated from an exceedingly dead German, apparently a fairly senior officer, who had evidently been there for some little time. I ordered one of my teams to clear him out, and returned to the trench. A few minutes later the corporal of the team emerged looking green in the face. "Excuse me, Sir," he said, "but the men don't like the job much, the old gentleman is falling to pieces." I replied: "Listen, corporal, I have been down the whole of the East Surreys' line. There is only one other decent dugout in it, which is now their headquarters. If the men are so lady-like that they can't clear away a dead Hun, I am not going to make them. But, you can tell them that if they don't, they will have the choice of spending the night with the old gentleman, just as he is, or outside in the trench in the snow. I shall be all right at the East Surrey headquarters." The corporal descended into the dugout with an armful of sang bags, and I soon heard the sound of the spades again, accompanied by shouts of "'ere comes 'is leg Bill", "nice bit of leather", "look at 'is – medals" and so on. Their efforts were well rewarded, for behind the spot where the old gentleman had been, there was a store of red wine, pumpernickel, and several tins of Teutonic delicacies. The dugout was thoroughly cleaned and disinfected, and we spent a most comfortable evening enjoying all this excellent food. To avoid any contretemps, I took over the wine, mulled it, and handed out generous portions to the men. A good time was had by all.

Next day was fairly quiet, but for two serious casualties. My servant, Private Archer, was badly hit while taking down a message to the rear. He got back to England, and I received one long and very touching letter from him. I wrote several times to him but got no further reply, and I am fairly certain that he died of his wound. I missed him badly, for I was very fond of him. Never, before or since, have I received such faithful services as I did from him. He looked after my clothes, cooked my meals and even darned my socks with the greatest efficiency. He had been a fisherman at Lowestoft before the war, and he darned socks as if he were mending a fishing net. My mother always said that she could never compete with him in this respect. He was always at hand to accompany me around the trenches at night, utterly fearless of danger, and if I did not happen to need him he would be waiting up for me with a hot drink when I came off duty.

The other casualty was my old friend Lieutenant-Colonel Alfred Irwin. He was hit in the leg and lay out in a shell hole. An officer started to get to him, but was ordered back by him. Later on the officer tried again, but Irwin said he was quite comfortable in the shell hole, and that the officer was not to risk his life, so he stayed there all day in the snow. That was absolutely typical of Irwin, a great soldier and a very brave man.

At this time I was still a Second-Lieutenant and junior officer in the battery, so it was with much surprise that I received a message from Captain McIver the following morning, saying that he and another of the battery officers were sick and would be evacuated, while the third officer had been wounded. I was now in command of the battery, which was to be relieved that night. I assumed that it was merely a temporary arrangement, as McIver had no power to decide who was to succeed him. The division was duly relieved, and the battery was billeted in a large farm not far from Abbeville and near the little town of Aine. It was the best billet we ever encountered. For some reason we were the first British troops ever to be billeted there. The farmer employed several hands, of both sexes, and they all made us most welcome, so that friendships soon began to spring up. Some of these developed into warm attachments during the seven weeks that we were lucky enough to spend there. When we finally left, there were many tears from the girls and kisses all round, and our hand carts were loaded with gifts of butter, eggs and cream, including an enormous surprise parcel for the officers, only to be disclosed after we had left. For several months afterwards a brisk correspondence was carried on in a weird mixture of English and French between the men and these kind and warm-hearted people.

On 19 December, which happened to be my 21st birthday, I was summoned to brigade headquarters by the brigade major. He began the interview by telling me that it had been decided that I should have permanent command of the 55th Trench Mortar Battery, so that I was now a Captain. When I had recovered from this shock, he handed me a copy of the day's Army Orders, saying that he thought it might interest me. I learned that I had been awarded a Military Cross (M.C.), the first in the battery, with the following citation:

> For conspicuous gallantry in action. He fought his trench guns with great courage and skill, killing 42 of the enemy. Later, he fired one of his guns from a shell hole in front of the position, and thereby caused 40 of the enemy to surrender.

It seemed to be an exaggeration, but, after all, I had not recommended myself for the medal, and maybe I counted wrong. The brigade major concluded the interview with a charming gesture. He took a small length of M.C. ribbon from his pocket and gave it to me, saying that he knew how difficult it was to obtain it in these parts. I returned to the battery feeling as if I was walking on air.

On my return, I went to the men's quarters to inspect their dinners. I found them enjoying excellent plum duff, and remarked to the cooks that it was better than what our cook served up in the officers' mess. In the afternoon my new servant, Private Wade, sewed the M.C. ribbon on my tunic. During dinner that evening I was told that some of the men were outside and would like to have a word with me. This was unusual, because any interviews between the men and myself had to be arranged through the intermediary of the battery sergeant major or one of the sergeants. However I went out to find six grinning men, headed by a certain Private Windsor, who was holding an object wrapped in paper. "Beg pardon, Sir," said the latter, "we heard that your cook doesn't know how to make plum duff so (presenting the parcel with a flourish) the men thought you might like a bit of theirs." Then with a broad smile: "And, Sir, they all want to congratulate you on your M.C." I burst out laughing, thanked them, and away they went. That was just like the old 55th Trench Mortar Battery. Their discipline, according to army standards, was deplorable and they dearly loved a chance of pulling the officer's leg. But I preferred it that way. We had been through the fire together, and had become comrades and friends. I went to bed that night a very happy man.

Two days later Army Orders appeared and we found that two Distinguished Conduct Medals and eleven Military Medals had been awarded to men still with the battery, and a further four or five to some who had become casualties. For our size we must have been the most decorated unit in the British army.

By this time, there were few officers and men still serving with the division, who, like myself, had come to France with it originally. All these battalions and other fighting units were now being built up afresh. One of the important changes was the promotion of the divisional commander Major-General Sir Ivor Maxse, who was given command of the XVIII Corps with the rank of lieutenant-general.

Maxse's place was taken by Major-General Sir Richard Lee, a very different type of man. He was a very experienced Royal Engineer and staff officer. He had followed along with General Sir Hubert Gough, first as Chief Royal Engineer of a division, then of a corps. He had been Chief Engineer of Fifth Army under Gough before coming to the 18th (Eastern) Division. He was undoubtedly a very clever man, with a wide knowledge of the Art of War, as he was to prove later on. He was also the most brilliant reader of maps that I have ever encountered. I was to know him at fairly close quarters, and, with due respect for his ability, it always seemed to me that he lacked a great deal on the human side of his job. It was not that he was cruel or heartless; he was just not interested in the human side of his men, and was seldom to be seen in the line. As a result, he never understood how much they could or could not do. Nor did he realise how much more they could and would have done if he had known how to treat them and inspire them in the way that "the black man" Maxse used to do.

I once had to be at divisional headquarters during an 18th (Eastern) Division attack, which, incidentally, was extremely successful. Lee remained all day in his operations room, seated before an enormous map on which quantities of little flags were set out. Orders and messages were coming in every few minutes. Having read each one, he would pause for a few moments, thoughtfully move some of the little flags backwards or forwards, dictate more orders, and wait. It was like watching an expert chess player or, better still, a cunning old spider sitting in the middle of his web, pulling a few strands in or out, and waiting for his victims to make the inevitable mistake and come into his parlour.

It was not easy to build up the battery again, but I started with two big advantages. The first was that, although I was the only officer left, I still had a fair sprinkling of the original old hands among the other ranks, including some non-commissioned officers. Secondly, the battery enjoyed a good reputation in the brigade, a reputation which it never lost, and, indeed, increased during the last year of the war. This made my work considerably easier than it might otherwise have been. All my new officers and men came from the infantry battalions of the brigade. I had a talk with all the four battalion commanders to explain what kind of men I needed. Their record of "crimes" did not interest me at all, except of course for cases of cowardice. I was glad to have misfits, men who had got on the wrong side of their officers, or who could never get used to "square bashing," but they had to be strong, brave in battle and possessing of initiative. If unsuitable men were sent, they would be returned. If these lieutenant-colonels would send me the right kind of men for my purposes, I would do my best to see that the battery would continue to render to the battalions the same assistance and co-operation as it had tried to give in the past. The lieutenant-colonels responded very fairly to my appeal, and, in point of fact, I only had to return one man to his battalion, for indiscipline, during the two years in which I commanded the battery. I returned none of the officers that were sent to me, although there was one of whom I had doubts, and whom I might have sent back, had not the armistice occurred.

The other officers were a splendid lot. The first to come was young Lieutenant Douglas Sutherst, the boy from the 7th West Kents whom I had first met in front of the mound in the Schwaben Redoubt. Unfortunately he was only with us for six months, and then had to leave. His battalion, and he with it, was transferred to the 53rd Brigade. He ended up in command of the 53rd Trench Mortar Battery, with a well-earned M.C. The next was Captain Frederick Gaywood, a first-rate officer in every respect. He was with the battery for fifteen months, winning an M.C., and, after the German attack in March 1918, returned to his battalion where experienced officers were very badly needed. Here he won a bar to his M.C., and remained in the army as a regular after the war. The others – including a few who were only with the battery for a short time – were all first-rate Stokes-gun officers. They were brave men who knew their jobs, and, although very different in their characters, all utterly loyal. We were all friends and it was a pleasure and a privilege to be in command of them. I had the same feeling about the men, and I know that all who served in the battery felt it too be a happy unit.

Coming, as they did, from four different battalions, the men were a mixed lot with plenty of individualists among them, but newcomers soon settled down and seemed to be proud of their new unit.

I used to have a talk with all newcomers to the battery. I told them they would find life in the battery rather different to what it had been in their respective battalions. When they had learned the proper use of the Stokes guns, they would become specialists like the rest of the battery. We treated them as men, able to look after their bodies and their weapons, and not as children who could not be trusted to do anything without continuous parades and inspections. The result would be fewer parades, provided they kept up a proper standard of smartness and efficiency, because, after a rough time in the line, we wanted them to rest and enjoy themselves as much as possible. The fewer men I had appearing before me on a charge, the better I would be pleased. I expected them to behave themselves when out of the line, but, if they had to do silly things, they should at least have the sense to see that I didn't know about them. I explained that I expected the men to fight when in the trenches. They might often find themselves without an officer or non-commissioned officer to tell them what to do, I said. If that happened, they must be active and do something, and not sit about waiting for orders. When in doubt, they must always remember Major-General Maxse's slogan: "Kill Germans". This was all very unorthodox but it seemed to me the only common-sense way of treating a small unit of this sort.

The only man I ever returned to his unit was a certain Private Pepper, a very tough customer, but a first-rate fighting soldier. One evening, hearing an unholy row in the men's quarters, I sent a recently-joined subaltern to stop it. He found a riotous game of housey in progress, presided over by Pepper, and told the men to make less noise. Pepper turned to him and told him to go away, using the unprintable army term. He was promptly put under arrest and came before me next morning. On hearing the evidence I told him I was not going to deal with the case. I had no use for men like him in the battery, so he would be returned to his battalion and would come before the lieutenant-colonel. His offence, insolence to an officer, was an extremely serious one from the army's point of view. I spoke to the lieutenant-colonel about the case beforehand. When Pepper was brought before him, the latter, on hearing the evidence, asked him whether he would accept his summary punishment or go for court-martial. Pepper, wisely, agreed to the former, and was sentenced to 28 days' Field Punishment No. 1. Pepper bore no grudge whatever. Some weeks later I came across him on sentry duty in the front line. "'ow are you, Sir?" he enquired, "nice to see you again. 'ow's the battery?, wish I was back with them." We parted the best of friends.

VIII

Episodes and Events

Early 1917

We returned to the trenches at the end of January 1917, to the right of, and beyond Desire Trench, opposite the village of Miraumont on the River Ancre. There was very little activity, and after a few days the calm, apart from some desultory artillery fire, became almost uncanny. Patrols began to find some of the German trenches unoccupied. We moved on, little by little, and eventually it was clear that the Germans had begun to retreat. They tried to fight a delaying action at Irles, a strong point on a hill, but another brigade in the 18th (Eastern) Division cleared them out, taking 400 prisoners. Then the pursuit began, and it was interesting to see our formations moving up, with outposts, piquets and main body. Owing to the German retreat, the line was shortening so that, soon afterwards, we were "squeezed out" and withdrawn, moving to a very quiet sector of the line in front of Bethune, where we stayed for a few weeks.

From tactical and strategical points of view, the German retreat was a very clever move. With great deliberation they retreated to a previously prepared and extremely strong system of trenches called the Hindenburg Line, from 10–40 miles to the east of their old positions. The Hindenburg Line was an elaborate affair, very carefully sited, with belts of barbed wire 10–20 yards wide. Below the trench was an underground tunnel running for miles, with bays, in which defenders lived, and numerous barricades. The whole system was fitted with electric light. All the ground between their new and old positions had been sown with booby traps, and utterly devastated. All trees, even fruit trees, had been cut down, and little towns like Bapaume, Pèronne and St. Quentin had been destroyed. It was a splendid opportunity for these barbarous Teutons ... to indulge their passion for what they call *Schadenfreude* (meaning pleasure derived from another's misfortune). Outside Pèronne they had put up a large notice board, now at the Imperial War Museum, with the inscription: "*Nicht ärgern, nur wundern*" (Don't be angry, just be amazed).

There were three excellent reasons for the German retreat. First, their lines on the Somme and in the River Ancre valley had become untenable after their final loss of Thiepval and the Poziéres ridge. Second, their new line was considerably shorter than the old one. Their third reason was somewhat more subtle; the French Commander-in-Chief, old Marshal Joseph 'Papa' Joffre, had been '*limogé*', or 'bowler hatted' as we say in England, nowadays. His place had been taken by General Robert Nivelle, who had earned a big reputation at Verdun. The latter was preparing a large offensive which, so he said, would inevitably bring about the final victory. No secret whatsoever had been made of his intentions, and the Germans had detailed knowledge of his plans. Now the German retreat to the Hindenburg Line put these plans completely out of joint. In spite of this, Nivelle persisted in launching his great offensive, without altering his plans. As might be expected, these resulted in a costly failure, although not so costly as some of the efforts of his predecessor, old Joffre. This was the reason for the serious mutinies that broke out in several French regiments, and rendered the French army more or less impotent for the rest of 1917.

From the German point of view, the only thing that could be said against their retreat was that armies seldom carry out these movements to the rear, when they are confident of victory, and it cannot have been good for their morale.

In March 1917, I was in London on leave and, to please my parents, decided to attend one of the distributions of medals carried out by the King George V at Buckingham Palace. My mother, in great excitement, bought herself a new hat for the occasion, and insisted on accompanying me. She, poor dear, doubtless imagined that she, and all the other proud mothers, would be entertained to cosy 'elevenses' by the Queen Mary, or perhaps Princess Mary, while His Majesty was handing out the medals to their sons. Disillusion awaited her, for, when our taxi arrived at the Palace, she was left to stand outside the railings in the rain, while I was ushered indoors by a flunkey. I was led upstairs into a large ante room with its walls covered with pictures of Queen Victoria's family, mostly in groups, by Winterhalter and similar artists, together with spirited and gory battle scenes of the Victorian era. There must have been 200–300 officers standing about, for the room contained no seating accommodation whatsoever, in spite of the fact that many of those present had lost a limb or were using crutches. We all hung about for an hour after the appointed time. Then, a functionary, it may have been the Lord Chamberlain, put in an appearance. He lined us up in Indian file, and gave us minute instructions as to how to behave on entering the presence of His Majesty. The latter would be standing on a dais in the next room. We were to approach him, halt, bow, have the medal attached by him, offer a hand (with the glove off, most important), turn half left and march to the other door. Another half hour went by, and then things began to happen. In the distance, a voice was repeating some words again and again at great speed. At first the words were indistinguishable; it might almost have been a bookmaker shouting "Two to one the field, two to one the field!" Then, as I got nearer, I made out the words gabbled together at top speed were "I am very pleased to present you with the Military Cross." No doubt His Majesty, like the rest of us, wanted his lunch, and in view of his late arrival was making up for lost time.

The boy in front of me had lost an arm and a leg, and hobbled towards the dias with much difficulty. His Majesty, to do him justice, interrupted his incantations and talked very kindly to him, asking him if he was being well looked after at Roehampton. I followed. The King took one look at me and started off again, "I am very pleased to present you with the Military Cross." For some absurd reason, I was in an appalling state of nerves at the imminent prospect of shaking hands with the King. I completely forgot the Lord Chamberlain's admonitions, and in all probability disgraced myself by forgetting to remove my glove, and bowing at the wrong time. However, I arrived at the other doorway to find my Military Cross safety attached to my tunic by a sort of picture hook. An attendant standing on the other side of the door promptly whipped the medal off, and placed it in a blue-leather case, which he handed to me. Then I was hustled briskly down another staircase out into the rain to where my mother was waiting outside the railings.

The ceremony could hardly be described as inspiring. Most of the officers present were young enough to still retain a little sentiment in their make-up, and a little consideration, perhaps a chair and a cup of coffee while waiting, and a few personal words from his Majesty, would have proved a never-to-be-forgotten experience. After all, we had been assured by Lord Kitchener that "Your King and Country Need You," and everyone there had given proof that they had undergone great danger, and had given their best to serve him. I can now sympathise with His Majesty when I read, in his biography by Harold Nicholson, that, during the war, he invested no less than 50,000 officers and men. Perhaps some other members of the Royal Family might have been pressed into service to lighten his burden? Certainly the Prince of Wales would have been much more usefully employed in a duty of this kind, rather than visiting the trenches, thereby causing considerable worry to those who were entrusted with his safety. In any case this one experience was enough for me, and when later on I was invited to attend another investiture, I declined.

At the end of April 1917, the 18th (Eastern) Division went into the line in front of Arras, opposite the Village of Chérisy, which formed part of the Hindenburg Line. Earlier in the month, Third Army under then General and later Field Marshal Edmund Allenby had launched a large attack in conjunction with Nivelle's great "end the war" offensive on the Chemin des Dames, which, in comparison with our previous attacks, was considered quite successful. In order to exploit these gains, another great attack was launched on 3 May, on a front from Lens to the River Ancre. In *The 18th Division in the Great War*, the author, Captain G.H.F. Nichols, with his usual talent for understatement, describes it as a political battle undertaken to remove the German pressure on the French. He added that it might even be termed a rash operation, at any rate on the Chérisy front. The attack failed all along the line.

The 18th's part in it can only be described as an irresponsible fiasco, shockingly planned, badly carried out, and badly fought. The division was put in the line only three days before the attack, and had no time to get acquainted with the lay of the country. The attack was launched at 3.45 a.m. in pitch darkness. The 54th Brigade, on the right of the 55th Brigade, after covering 500 yards, ran into a thick belt of wire that had not been destroyed in the artillery preparation. The 55th Brigade (8th East Surreys on the left, 7th Buffs on the right) reached their first objective. The latter group remained for some time and fought off some small counter attacks. Later, with both flanks in the air, they were ordered back to the first objective. Then the Germans launched a strong counter attack, admirably supported by their artillery. At this moment – nobody knows how it happened – an order to retire was passed down the line.

Two of my Stokes guns had gone forward with each battalion, while I remained in our original front line with the other four guns to be used wherever they might be needed. Both the forward sections arrived at their final objective with the infantry. The section on the right with the 7th Buffs went into action and knocked out a German machine gun, and eventually withdrew with the infantry. On the left, the guns also reached their destination, fired over 50 rounds and silenced some machine guns but, on their way back, the whole of one gun team was killed by a single shell, although the officer with them escaped.

Having seen the two forward sections on their way, I awaited developments in the darkness. Messages began to arrive saying that good progress was being made, and all appeared to be going well, although I noticed that very few groups of prisoners seemed to be coming down. No messages were received asking for additional guns or ammunition to be sent forward. Day dawned with a clear sky and the hot sun beating down. The artillery fire lessened, but still there was no definite news from the line. Suddenly the German shell fire increased and seemed to be getting much nearer. Someone on the ridge in front of me shouted and I went up to see what was going on. I had the shock of my life. As far as I could see on either side, thousands of our men were returning, wave after wave, towards me. It seemed as if the whole British army was on the run. German shells were bursting among them in a heavy barrage, steadily moving onwards. I had my reserve guns ready to fire but there was nothing for them to do. Our men crowded in their thousands into our original front line, and much of the rest of the day was spent in sorting them out, while the Germans made no attempt to advance beyond their old front line, which, at this point, was well out of range of my guns. The Germans opposing us were first-class troops who knew their business. They put in their counter attack at exactly the right moment and the co-ordination between their infantry and artillery, helped by star-shell signals, was masterly. Had they pressed their counter attack further, there would have been little to stop them.

A long time afterwards, in a German newspaper, I came across an account of this battle written by one of the German officers who had taken part. It was very fair and factual and not in the least boastful. It appeared that they had knowledge that the attack would take place, and had worked out their tactics beforehand. They had left only a few "die hard" sentries in their front line to meet the attack, and this accounted for the small number of prisoners that we captured.

It might have been thought that sufficient muddles had been perpetrated during this day's fighting, but there were still more to come. Apparently the divisional headquarters had never received word that the men of the 8th East Surreys and 7th Buffs, who had arrived at the final objective, were now back in our front line. Consequently the 7th Queens were ordered to carry out another completely pointless attack, in order to relieve them. One company, reinforced by a support company, made a little progress but eventually had to return to their trenches because the other two companies of the battalion had not been able to advance owing to heavy machine-gun fire. In the circumstances – at 7.15 p.m., in broad daylight – it was sheer murder to order such an attack.

The country round Chérisy – with gently sloping downs, firm soil and a complete absence of obstacles – would have been ideal for tank warfare. It is hardly necessary to mention that as far as our part of the front was concerned, no tanks were sent into action. Perhaps that was because High Command were holding them in reserve for use in the next great slaughter at Passchendaele in July, when the hundreds that were sent into action were quite unable to operate and merely got bogged down in the mud?

Following the Chérisy battle, the division remained in the line for another month, and, after a few weeks' rest in the back areas, moved up to Dickebusch, a ruined village not far behind the front line in the Ypres Salient.

IX

Mud and Shellfire at Ypres

1917

The 'Red Hats' at G.H.Q. never took the trouble to
visit the line in order to find out what the conditions
were really like. Had those staff officers done so, they
might have discovered that the Ypres Salient was the
most unsuitable part of the whole line in which to
undertake a great offensive. To explain why this was so,
it is necessary to give a brief description of the situation
as it was at that time. The salient was in the form of an
arc pushing towards the German lines, with Ypres near
the centre of its base. The German front line lay on a
slight ridge, well above our positions. Ten years later, I
walked over this ground and realised, for the first time,
the fact that the Germans had had a perfect bird's-eye
view of everything that went on in the salient.

In the salient it was impossible to dig deeper than
two or three feet into the ground, except in one or two
places, because water seeped in. Consequently our
line consisted of barricades built up with sand bags,
so there were very few shelters of any kind in which
the men could rest. For the same reason, artillery had
to be placed in the open with little or no protection,
always in the close vicinity of a road, because, owing to
the state of the ground, it would otherwise have been

impossible to bring up their ammunition and supplies. Since the Second Battle of the Ypres in 1915, the sector had been fairly quiet and the Germans had used the time in building pillboxes at every part of their positions. These edifices, large and small, were made of reinforced concrete and were impervious to shell fire from field artillery; the shells simply bounced off them and it took a direct hit from heavy artillery to send one of them into the air, as occasionally happened.

In these circumstances it was not possible to conceal our preparations (not that any attempt was made to do so) and, not unnaturally, the Germans brought up all available artillery; during the whole period of the battle and its preparation, they bombarded all these innumerable sitting targets by day and night, so that life became almost equally dangerous whether we were in the forward positions or not.

The principal crossroads in the British area were known as Shrapnel Corner and Hellfire Corner. Every night terrible and wonderful scenes occurred at them. The Germans gunners had the ranges exactly for these crossroads, and salvoes would fall on them at intervals of a minute or a half a minute. By the flash of the guns in the vicinity, one could see the limbers bumping across, the horses or mules at full gallop, and drivers desperately using their whips in the hope of getting across before the next German salvo crashed down. Every morning there would be a litter of smashed limbers, stores, shells, and dead men, horses and mules piled up in confusion.

As if these horrors were not enough, there then came a deluge of rain. It began to rain on the late evening of 31 July, the first day of the Third Battle of

Ypres, which was in 1917. Rain continued to pour down in torrents, almost without a break, for the next four days, and the weather remained appalling for the rest of the year. The Germans, on the higher ground, were less affected by it than we were. On our side of no-man's-land, there were numerous little streams, tributaries of the Yser River, which, owing to the incessant artillery fire, and swollen by the rain, burst through courses and turned the whole area into one vast quagmire. As time went on, the only way of reaching the line at all was by using the wooden duckboards, of which many miles had been laid down. These were perfect targets for the German artillery. If a man carrying up stores happened to become detached from his party and slipped off the greasy duckboards, he stood an excellent chance of drowning in one of the enormous, rain-filled shell holes. Many losses occurred for this reason alone.

In view of these conditions, it is not difficult to understand that these offensive operations in the salient were exceedingly hazardous, and should never have been commenced in the first place. After the first day's negligible results, followed by four days of incessant rain, it might be thought that anyone but a set of blood-thirsty lunatics would have called off the whole thing. Indeed, in the middle of August, General Sir Hubert Gough, the commander of the Fifth Army, asked G.H.Q. for permission to break off the operation. But the armchair warriors of G.H.Q. and Whitehall went on with their planning right into October, sending up one division after another to be destroyed. Operations didn't cease until November. All this time the English newspapers were publishing tales of great victories and enormous casualties inflicted on the enemy. At the end of these operations we had advanced four or five miles across a desert of shell holes.

On 13 July, the 18th (Eastern) Division went into the line of the south of the salient between Sanctuary Wood and the Menin Road. The 55th Trench Mortar Battery and other troops of the 55th Brigade, 2000 in all, spent the next 18 days carrying up ammunition and stores to the front line, and digging various emplacements and field works. It was a horrible experience. The Germans, fully aware of our preparations, brought up more artillery every day, and shelled our back areas mercilessly. With great observation from their positions, they created havoc among our working parties and among the guns standing wheel to wheel, and without protection, all round the banks of Zillebeke Lake. Out of the 2000 men constituting the working parties, 864 became casualties, almost all from shell fire. This prolonged ordeal intensified as the days went by and was extremely bad for morale. To use a modern army expression we were all completely "browned off" and no one had any illusions as to what would be in store for us when the battle began.

On 31 July, the assault was carried out by the 53rd and 54th Brigades, which were supposed to leap-frog through the 30th Division after the latter had reached the first objective. Unfortunately, the 30th, mistaking their objective, had veered to the left, so that our two brigades had to attack the pillboxes in the German front line without any artillery support, for the barrage supporting the infantry's advance had, by this time, lifted. At the cost of appalling casualties, they succeeded in advancing about 1000 yards. When the rain came down in torrents that evening, the whole area became a mass of waterlogged shell holes in which thousands of corpses were floating.

The 55th Brigade was kept in reserve near Dickebusch on 31 July. We spent a miserable day watching the ambulances and walking wounded returning from the front line and listening to harrowing accounts of the slaughter that was taking place in the attack. Mercifully we were not ordered to move up.

On 4 August, the 55th Brigade went into the line. One battalion, the 7th Queens, took part in an assault with battalions of the 54th Brigade. A little ground was gained, and at the end of the day almost all were back in the line from which they had started. In view of this, the remainder of the 55th Brigade stayed all day in the front-line positions in Sanctuary Wood and incurred many more casualties without being drawn into the assault. On 17 August, what was left of the division – worn out and dispirited – left the line and went into rest billets near Wormhoudt.

In August, a change occurred in the command of the 55th Brigade with the departure of Brigadier-General George "Dicky" Price, and the arrival of his successor, Brigadier-General Edward Wood. One of his first actions was to ask the battalion commanders, Major Hector Heyland, O.C. the 55th Machine-Gun Company, and myself to dinner. This was quite unprecedented for, up to then, a mutual and very strong feeling existed between the unit commanders and brigade headquarters that the less they saw of one another, the better. At this, our first meeting, Brigadier-General Wood made a very great impression on us all, and, the more I got to know him, the more genuine affection and admiration I felt for him. He was a well-built, good-looking man, red faced, with penetrating blue eyes. He was quite unlike any brigadier-general I had ever met. Had the other British generals possessed one half of his qualities, the war would have been won in half the time. He was far from being a master of subtle tactics, and his knowledge of map reading was somewhat limited, as I found out, to my cost, later on. But these defects, oddly enough, proved to be of little importance, because his brigade majors, Major Randolph Chell and Captain Charles Runge, and his Staff Captain, Bertie Keown, looked after all the tactical and administrative work with supreme confidence and efficiency.

The brigade was never better handled and managed than during Brigadier-General Wood's regime. Both Chell and Keown had learned their business the hard way: the former as a subaltern and later adjutant of the 10th (Service) Battalion, The Essex Regiment, the latter as a subaltern in the 7th Buffs. Both of them were in their twenties; with their brains and competence, they were typical examples of what the best of Kitchener's Army young officers could do, if given the opportunity. Brigadier-General Wood, although far from stupid, was a very simple man. He held very strongly to the old-fashioned idea that it was the duty of a military leader to lead his men, literally, into battle, and that is precisely what he did himself. He was utterly without fear, and simply ignored danger, as he ignored other unpleasant things that came his way.

When the brigade was in the line, Brigadier-General Wood's headquarters were always situated well forward, and he would spend very day striding round the trenches, carrying an enormous cavalry lance with a pennant and smoking a long cigar. When a battle was in progress, he was always to be found in the thick of it, obviously enjoying himself, and anyone who happened to accompany him on these occasions could be sure that there would never be a dull moment in the proceedings. At the time of his appointment, during the Ypres offensive, the morale of the brigade was far from high. The men had been muddled about disgracefully at Chérisy, and the lives of many of them had been thrown away uselessly. The prospect of the future holocausts in the Ypres Salient was far from inviting. In these circumstances, Brigadier-General Wood was the finest possible type of man to take over the brigade. The men grinned when they saw his familiar figure strolling round the trenches and they went into battle with him in good heart, having made up their minds that what was good enough for the "old man" was good enough for them.

Wood was extremely wise in his treatment of his battalion and other unit commanders. They were all most capable men, who had learnt their business in battle. Every one of them had earned one or more awards in combat. The brigadier-general realised their quality, trusted them, and never fussed them. He merely told them what they had to do and left them to do it in their own way. Although he never openly criticised his superiors, he detested red tape, and either ignored it or blandly avoided it, if it got in his way. Thus, we soon found out that brigade headquarters would grant all our reasonable requests, if it was humanly possible to do so, whether or not they were provided for by army regulations or authorised by High Command.

Although the brigadier-general was a dignified figure, he was always kind and considerable to us, even in quite small matters. On one occasion, during a battle, the mail arrived, including a quarter-pound tin of tobacco – a commodity that we had been without for a week – for him. There were five of us present, and the general promptly emptied his tin on to the table and divided the tobacco into six equal parts, retaining one for himself. Not unnaturally, he soon became extremely popular; we all laughed affectionately at his foibles and adventures, but we all served him to the best of our ability.

At our first meeting, at Wood's dinner-party for his various unit commanding officers, I was to experience his quality. Major Heyland, O.C. of 55th Machine-Gun Company, and one of my best friends, was feeling very pleased with himself, for he was going to Paris next day for four days' leave. He was showing me his leave warrant, and I was expressing my envy. The brigadier-general overheard this and said to me: "Why don't you go too?" I replied that unfortunately I had no leave warrant. "We can soon put that right," returned the general, "Keown (turning to the Staff Captain) make out a leave warrant for Heath to go to Paris with Heyland tomorrow." This seemed too good to be true, for leave warrants, on printed forms, were only issued by division, and the brigadier-general had no right to issue them, nor was brigade in possession of the printed forms. However, Keown wrote out an order saying that the General O.C. 55th Infantry Brigade desired me to accompany Major Heyland on leave to Paris, covered it with important-looking rubber stamps and the general signed it. What is more, it worked! Armed with this order, I got by all the Military Police, and spent a glorious four days in Paris with Heyland.

Early in October, the division returned again to the salient, the object being to capture the village of Poelcapelle, which was in the vicinity of Passchendaele. The 55th Brigade was to lead the attack, and, as usual before these battles, the brigadier-general held a conference of his commanders to issue orders and co-ordinate plans. That conference was a grim comedy. Every officer in the hut was a brave, experienced soldier, but each one knew perfectly well that, in the prevailing conditions, a successful attack was out of the question.

Once again the Germans, in their pillboxes, had perfect observation over our lines. Moreover, the rain had been falling steadily for the previous month, and the whole area of attack was a morass of mud and water. To make matters worse, the battalions were now made up, for the most part, of raw recruits straight out from England, not properly accustomed, as yet, to their units and lacking any experience of warfare. Meanwhile, there we all were, discussing the timetable of arrival at the Blue Line, the Green Line and all the other objectives all knowing full well that the sole result would be another large casualty list with nothing to show for it. When all this had been discussed, an incident occurred for which I shall never cease to owe the deepest gratitude to the brigadier-general. He turned to me and said: "And what do you propose to do in this show, Heath, with your Stokes guns?" I stood up: "I'll try to do whatever you tell me to, Sir," I replied, "but, since you ask me, frankly I do not consider I can do anything useful at all. I do not see how any man, however strong, can be expected to carry over 70 pounds' weight of gun or shells through that mud outside." The brigadier-general looked thoughtfully at me, and then said quietly: "You are quite right. Your battery is not to take part in this battle." So we stayed out, and I thanked God that a sensible and humane brigadier-general was in command of the brigade.

The attack was a complete failure, as we had all foreseen. The 54th Brigade on our right made a little ground and got halfway to the objective. The 55th Brigade made a minute advance but had to return to the original line after losing a great many men. It should, however, be mentioned that later on the 53rd Brigade succeeded in capturing Poelcapelle in a most ingenious way. Our line ran roughly in the shape of an angle. On one side of this, a few men were in position carrying "pole targets". These consisted of poles to which were attached pieces of wood roughly shaped to represent the outline of a soldier lying down, facing the enemy. These pole targets were used normally for giving recruits practice in rapid rifle fire. The other angle of the line was manned by the troops carrying out the attack. At Zero hour, the pole target carriers got busy, pushing the targets up and down for dear life. The German front line troops mistook them for the attackers, and turned all their fire on to them. When the efforts of the defence were fully engaged in the wrong direction, the real attackers emerged from the other angle of our line, and managed to cross no-man's-land and overcome the German defenders before the latter knew what had hit them. The credit for this attack belongs to the 53rd Brigade's commander, Brigadier-General Harold Higginson. Needless to say, he had the greatest difficulty in obtaining the consent of High Command to carry it out. No publicity was given to this outstanding little success, so that the Germans never learned how they had lost Poelcapelle, at least until the war was over. Incidentally, my views about the folly of attempting to use Stokes guns in this waterlogged ground were proved to be correct. The 53rd Trench Mortar Battery, with the utmost effort, managed to drag a couple of guns and a few rounds of ammunition over to Poelcapelle, and then found it impossible to fire at all as both guns and shells were completely steeped in mud and water.

After Poelcapelle, the 55th Brigade spent the next five weeks in and out of the front line opposite Houthulst Forest, to the north of the Ypres Salient. It was a dreary, miserable experience. Our front line was the road running along the edge of the forest, which by now was a scattered collection of broken tree stumps, and, as usual, the whole of our positions were under observation. My guns were situated in two old German pillboxes on the road, and I could only visit them by night. The only way of reaching the front line was to stumble along the wooden duckboard tracks laid along the edges of the enormous shell holes. The

German artillery had the range of these tracks and, every so often, would drop salvoes along them during the night, although the shelling was not nearly so severe as what we had had to undergo in July. The torrential rain gave way to hard frosts. The troops, of course, could not move about at all in the front line by day. This affected the circulation of their blood, so that there was a considerable outbreak of what was known as "trench foot". This was overcome, eventually, by the issue of long gumboots reaching to the thighs, and of supplies of whale oil. Rough and ready pedicure stations were established in the support lines for the use of those whose legs and feet showed signs of being affected. We left the salient a few days before Christmas to go into rest billets. We never were to go near this miserable hell on earth again.

The 55th Trench Mortar Battery spent a really memorable Christmas, and I enjoyed every minute of it. First came the ritual enormous midday dinner, with the officers serving and also drinking innumerable toasts with the men. When the effects had worn off a little, we fielded a side for a rugger match against our old friends the 55th Machine-Gun Company. It was the most hilarious match in which I had ever taken part. Only four or five on either side had ever played rugger before, so that the rules had to be explained as the game proceeded. The men soon got hold of the idea of tackling, and had the time of their lives practising the art on the officers, whether the latter had the ball or not. At the end of the game I was covered with bruises, and weak with laughter. In the evening we joined forces again with the machine gunners and held a concert in a large barn.

Captain Philip Heath

I had managed to borrow an ancient piano from one of the neighbouring farms, and this was hauled up into a huge farm wagon in the middle of the barn, into which the "artists" had to clamber to make their contributions. The officers had clubbed together for two large barrels of beer for the men who showed their appreciation by drinking them dry during the evening. Major Heyland, who arranged the programme, had insisted that all the officers of both units, should make some contribution to it. I am far from being a public entertainer, and have no singing voice whatsoever. However, I obliged by reciting "Christmas Day in the Workhouse". Much to my surprise, this was received with terrific cheering, so that I had to give an encore, the first somewhat bawdy story that came into my head.

During the whole war, one of the evergreen sources of jokes was plum-and-apple jam. This nauseous concoction, made of ingredients among which neither plums nor apples were particularly noticeable, was manufactured by the firm of Thomas Ticklers, who must have made a fortune out of it, judging by the frequency with which it appeared in the rations. We were all heartily sick of the stuff, and its appearance day after day in the ration bags was invariably greeted with sarcasm and booing. One of the men climbed on the wagon and sang a song about the jam with a catchy tune:

Tickler's Jam, Tickler's Jam,
'ow I loves old Tickler's Jam,
Plum and apple in one-pound pots,
Sent from England in ten-tonne lots,
Every night, when I'm asleep,

I'm dreaming that I am,
Sent up the line with the best of luck,
And Tommy Tickler's Jam

The men took it up with a will and insisted on two repeats, which must have been heard for miles around.

My last recollection of that evening was of one of my best battery officers and friends, Acting-Captain Stewart Bywaters, well lit up [i.e. under the influence of alcohol], standing on a table waving a fiddle. Heaven knows where he picked it up? He was playing brilliant improvisations before an admiring audience of orderlies and officers' servants, filling in the intervals between these items with a kind of serial, and equally brilliant, panegyric of everybody in the battery; and what a splendid lot we were, except, of course, for himself, the only blot on the landscape. Next morning he had no recollection whatever of his remarkable performance.

X

German Spring Offensive

March 1918

At the end of January 1918, the 18th (Eastern) Division moved south. The Oise River was now the boundary between the French and British armies. The 58th (2/1st London) Division was on the extreme south of the British lines at La Fère. Then came the 18th with the 14th (Light) Division on its left flank. It seemed an idyllic spot. The scenery was lovely. The Germans were at a comfortable distance on the other side of the River Oise and hardly a shot was fired for days on end. The only fly in the ointment was the great length of the divisional front, no less than 9500 yards to be covered by only 10 battalions. It had previously been decided to reorganise the army on a basis of three battalions to a brigade, instead of four as previously, with one pioneer battalion to each division. Thus, should the Germans decide to attack on our front, the results might be unpleasant.

Normally the River Oise would have constituted an excellent natural defence, but owing to a long spell of dry weather it could be crossed with little difficulty. There was no trench system. The front line consisted of a series of strong points together with some old forts, which were said to have been constructed by

Vauban. The 55th Trench Mortar Battery was busily engaged in making gun positions and stores of shells when I received an order to proceed, on 18 March, to Le Touquet. It seemed that it had been decided by G.H.Q. that a textbook on the proper use of Stokes guns was to be compiled, and one battery commander from each Army corps in the British army was to attend a conference, lasting a fortnight, to give the compilers of this work the benefit of their experience. We duly commenced our deliberations under an elderly colonel. On 21 March came the news that the Germans had launched a great offensive, but the colonel went placidly on with the business in hand, and a week went by before we were ordered to abandon the conference and proceed to Etaples where we were to await further orders.

Etaples was, as it were, the Clapham Junction of the British army. It was an enormous camp to which drafts from England, and men recovered from their wounds or illnesses who had been receiving treatment in the numerous hospitals in the neighbourhood, had to report. Here they were sorted out and dispatched in drafts to fill the strengths of the various battalions. It was a thoroughly bad system, although it was difficult to see how the problem could be dealt with differently. When a man arrived at Etaples, unless he was especially asked for by the C.O. of his battalion, he was liable to be sent off to join another battalion of the regiment to which he belonged. Thus a man of the 8th East Surreys, a battalion of which he was proud, where he felt at home among his friends and officers, might find himself in another East Surreys' battalion where he knew no one and with, possibly, another long spell in the Ypres

Salient to look forward. Etaples was detested by every soldier. While the men were awaiting their postings they were drilled, day after day, by a formidable collection of non-commissioned officers who, in their efforts not to lose their jobs and get sent up the line. These NCOs displayed the utmost zeal for spit and polish and, to put it bluntly, bullied their charges unmercifully. The guard rooms were always full.

Etaples was now in a somewhat chaotic state. Plenty of soldiers were arriving daily, men back from leave, drafts of reinforcements, casualties from the battle being carried to the hospitals. But none appeared to be leaving, for the harassed Railway Traffic Officers at the station had no idea as to the location of the various divisions. The Officers' Club was packed out, with three sittings at every meal, served by Women's Auxiliary Army Corps girls who did their best but were grossly overworked. The officers in charge of this great camp seemingly made no attempt to cope with the situation. Maybe they were worrying as to what their own fate might be if the Germans succeeded in reaching the coast.

Finally, in desperation, I decided to try to get back to the 18th (Eastern) Division without the blessing of the Etaples authorities. On the evening of 3 April, I went down to the station with my servant, Private Wade, and, without any papers, boarded a train that was said to be going somewhere up the line. Next morning the train pulled up at the station of Boves, about five miles from Amiens, and, looking out of the carriage window, I saw a man wearing the shoulder markings of a battalion of the 55th Brigade. We hastily left the train, and were directed to 8th East Surreys' headquarters, which was about 50 miles away from where I had left them.

When I found the 55th Brigade at Boves, it was but a shadow of its former self. The 8th East Surreys had been decimated. Before the German army's Spring Offensive, the battalion consisted of about 900 men and officers. Now there were about 90 left. Mercifully, Lieutenant-Colonel Alfred Irwin was alive and well, and I lived with him for a few days, for the 55th Trench Mortar Battery had completely disappeared. The guns had all been lost in the original front line posts in such places as Fort Vendeuil and Fort Liez. With such an enormous front to cover, Captain Frederick Gaywood, whom I had left in charge, had found it impossible to control the whole line. When the retreat began, the guns had to be left where they were, although many of our men had got away, and had been fighting as infantrymen. Gaywood had re-joined his old battalion, the East Surreys, and had done well. He was now commanding the remains of a company. Owing to Irwin's need for experienced officers, he gave up trench mortar work and remained with them.

Of the other officers, Captain Douglas Sutherst, the 7th West Kents' officer, now promoted, had had to follow his battalion to the 53rd Brigade, after the reorganisation of the brigades, and soon after was given command of the 53rd Trench Mortar Battery, which he was to lead with brilliance in the last months of the war, notably in the capture of the La Boisselle craters. Acting-Captain Stewart Bywaters was wounded but returned later on. Another officer had been killed and one was missing. The 55th Brigade had done its duty to the utmost, retreating under orders and fighting all the way as far as Pontoise, where the line was handed over to the French. After precisely one day's rest, they were bundled into French lorries and driven 40 miles straight into battle again to meet the German attack at Villers-Bretonneux. The 8th East Surreys had been at Marcelcave, just south of the village, and in all the fighting in this open country had lost only 2000 yards of ground, in spite of the overwhelming numerical odds against them. The High Command had no right to use up these exhausted troops in this way.

The 8th East Surreys had just come down from Marcelcave. They were utterly exhausted but their morale was as high as ever. They were proud of themselves and Irwin, with very good reason, was extremely proud of what they had done. Many of the men, indeed, had rather enjoyed the whole business, with the excitement and movement of what had amounted to open warfare, after the endless months of boredom and slaughter in the trenches. Moreover, the losses, although most severe, were not as serious as had appeared at first, for, as the days went by, men who were thought to be missing began to make their appearance. They had been caught up in the fighting with other units. Some had even been mixed up with the French. There were others who had been on leave and had been unable to return before, owing to the confusion and muddle at Etaples and on the railway. Even the High Command realised the futility of sending these troops into battle again without a long period of rest and training, except in the last extremity which, mercifully, never arose, for the Germans, as exhausted as our men, remained quiet for the next there weeks. There was one last engagement on this part of the line for the 18th (Eastern) Division. On 24 April, certain battalions, notably the 7th Queens and the 7th West Kents, fought all day, side by side with the French Foreign Legion and Lieutenant-General Sir John Monash's Australian Corps and, after a brilliant action, recaptured Villers-Bretonneux and Marcelcave. As usual, the credit for this was given to the Australians alone!

XI

Prelude to Victory

April–August 1918

For a short time I remained with the 8th East Surreys, in command of a company, but large reinforcements were coming in to bring the brigade up to strength and Brigadier-General Edward Wood told me to reform the 55th Trench Mortar Battery. Most of these reinforcements were youngsters fresh from England, and lacking in battle experience, but they settled down and soon became good fighting soldiers. Others were first-rate veterans, men who had recovered from wounds or had been transferred from other theatres of war like Palestine and Salonica.

One of the latter was a remarkable character. His name was Second-Lieutenant Oliver Madox Hueffer and he was a brother of Ford Madox Ford, the famous writer. He was a heavily built man, probably nearer fifty than forty years of age, but he was only a Second-Lieutenant. Heaven alone knows how he was allowed to be in the infantry at his age. As I had to leave the East Surreys so soon after his arrival, I had no opportunity to get to know him well, a fact that I infinitely regretted, for he was the best raconteur I had ever met, with his tales of the goings on in Salonica.

For once, the 18th (Eastern) Division was given the really adequate period of rest that it needed so badly in order to become once more a first-class fighting force. Until the end of June, as part of G.H.Q. Reserve, it was comfortably billeted in the Cavillon district. The programme of training was not unduly strenuous, and there was plenty of opportunity for fun and games. Of the latter, the chief attraction was the Divisional Show and Race Meeting.

The chief attraction of this race meeting was the mule race, one of the most hilarious items that I have ever had the privilege to watch, the more so as what happened was quite unexpected. There were 53 starters, and only four of them finished. The course was an oval, and the enormous field came into the final straight, bunched together and going well. Then things began to happen. Without warning, some of the mules on the outside edged steadily away to the left, until they were right off the course, and most of the others followed. The riders naturally did their best to steer them towards the winning post, but the mules either took no notice and went on their way, or, if the riders insisted, simply bucked them off to the delight of the crowd, which was nearly hysterical with laughter. The explanation was that, before the race, the mules had been tethered in lines about 100 yards from, and to the left of, the winning post. Evidently they had decided this new lark of running races was all very well in its way but enough was enough; it was time for them to return to their nose bags.

The army mules were most endearing animals when one got used to their ways, and their drivers became very fond of them. The mule is of course notorious for his obstinacy, but he, or it, is one of the most intelligent animals in creation, full of character and devilry and he possesses, what I firmly believe to be, a sense of humour. He is always ready with a playful nip for anyone who approaches unthinkingly, and some of the men swore that he can, and does, kick with his forelegs as well as his back legs. Mules are wonderfully sure footed, far more so than horses. The French used to take their mules, a much smaller variety, right up to the front line on the slippery duck boards carrying stores and ammunition. Mules are extremely hardy and excellent workers, but it is useless to overload them, for they simply go on strike.

Once, in a very quiet part of the line, the 8th East Surreys were being relieved by day, and all the companies were grouped under a hillside, waiting to march off. A double-limber wagon, heavily loaded, was standing in a quagmire of mud, with two mules harnessed to it. They tried their best, but could not move it. The rear portion was unlimbered, the mules tried again with the same result. Two other mules on a nearby wagon, which had been sardonically watching these operations, were unharnessed and re-harnessed in front of the mules on the first wagon. But, in spite of the prodding and cursing of the drivers, the single limber remained motionless. This time it was too much. Obviously the four mules could have moved the single limber, if they had wanted to, but they had decided to call it a day, and there they stood, with grins on their faces. The transport sergeant decided to put a stop to these unseemly goings on. He assembled a squad of men around the limber. At the word of command, they heaved it bodily into the air and on to the backs of the rear pair of astonished mules, and away they all went floundering through the mud amid the cheers and laughter of the battalion.

Another great attraction at this time was the Divisional Concert Party, which compared quite favourably with some of the other army and divisional Parties that were usually found performing at places like Poperinghe or Amiens. Ours always opened proceedings with the company seated, in pierrot costumes. Each performer would rise in turn and sing a verse of a topical song, with all of them joining in the chorus. Thus the Funny Man would jump from his chair, wink at the audience and begin:

> With a very nice girl that I met at Albert,
> I offered my love and my money to share.
> My money she took, but with repartee rare,
> "Your love I'll accept", she said, "*après la guerre*"

> With a hey-ho, lack a day, misery me
> And a *fol de rol', fol de rol le*.

This was greeted with cat calls. Everyone knew that no girl, let alone a very nice one, had put in an appearance in Albert for the last two years. Then there was 'Major-General Worthington,' who had apparently fought at Inkerman, and had won all his medals "for drinking up bottles of Worthington!" The best item, however, was the splendid old sketch *A Sister to Assist 'er!* It was played all over England for years, but now seems to be quite forgotten.

At the end of June, the division went into the line again, in the trenches facing the town of Albert.

It was a poor little place, even before its destruction by artillery. Its principal industry had consisted of a large bicycle factory. On the steeple of the modern and hideous Basilica, there was an enormous gold-coloured statue of the Virgin Mary holding the infant Jesus. It had been hit early in the war by a shell, and had assumed a horizontal position, being held from falling altogether by the heavy round base to which it was attached. Since then, the angle at which it hung had slowly decreased, and the statue now had its head pointing to the ground at an angle of nearly forty five degrees. There was a belief that when the statue finally toppled the war would come to an end.

This part of the line had now become fairly quiet, which gave us a chance to teach the new reinforcements how to do their job in the front line. Some small parties of Americans were sent up to spend a few days with us for instruction and, somewhat to our surprise, got along quite well with our men. Perhaps we were lucky, but these men were quiet, anxious to learn, and, if anything, too earnest and solemn. Their behaviour was in marked contrast to that which was generally ascribed to the American forces for, to put it mildly, the Yanks were not particularly popular with either with the British or the French armies at that time.

During this period in the line, an incident occurred for which I have never been able to find an explanation. One fine morning I entered a communication trench to get the front line. There was no particular activity, except for the heavy artillery on both sides engaged in counter-battery work. That is to say, each side was taking the guns of the other side as their target. There was a British aeroplane flying high, some distance away. I noticed that it was coming towards me, and appeared to be descending, with the engine, by the sound, running quite normally. As the plane approached at a height of about 1000 feet, I suddenly saw the body of the pilot emerge, roll over a few times in the air and finally fall to the ground a few yards from the trench in which I stood. The plane, with the engine apparently still working smoothly, plunged into the ground 100 yards away, where it was smashed to bits in the crash. It did not catch fire.

With Private Apted, my orderly, I got out of the trench and ran to where the pilot lay. He had died instantaneously, a young, very good looking boy with no outward sign of damage on his body, which we carried into the trench and then handed over to the stretcher bearers. I have never understood what caused this death; the weather was perfect, the plane seemed to be flying normally and no one was attacking it. Excluding the most unlikely possibility of suicide on the part of the pilot the only conjecture that I can make is that one of the shells, fired in the artillery counter battery work, may have passed, on its trajectory, through some vital part of the plane without exploding, and without hitting the engine. If so, it must have been an exceedingly rare occurrence.

During the period from the end of April to the end of July, the Somme front had been quiet. Towards the end of July the 55th Brigade was moved, a little to the right, into the trenches in front of the village of Morlancourt, where everything seemed to be comparatively quiet.

Captain Philip Heath

On 4 August, I went to a conference held by Brigadier-General Wood for commanding officers only, where we learned that a large offensive was planned to take place over a 20-mile front on 8 August. We were at the extreme left of the line, and our advance was to be comparatively small. This attack was to be a very different affair to the dismal slaughters of the past, for two most-important reasons. The first was that it would be led by no less than 450 tanks, with no preliminary bombardment, the infantry following close behind an intense creeping artillery barrage. Second, thank Heaven, the utmost secrecy was to be observed. The men would only be informed on the night before the battle. Naturally, the artillery strength was being heavily increased, but to avoid arousing the suspicions of the Germans, all the wheels of limbers coming up into position were being covered with straw, and prolonged bursts of machine gun fire would take place each night to drown any possible noise from this source and from the tanks moving up on the final night. The commanding officers returned to their units, which immediately became very busy, without the men knowing the reason for all the activity.

On the morning of the 6 August, I was awoken by a terrific uproar and someone came running into the dugout to say that the Huns had attacked, and were held up, a few hundred yards from my headquarters. I got up in record time, and went out to see what was going on. Apparently a local attack had been carried out by a contingent of *Sturm Truppen* (storm troops). These *Sturm Truppen* were carefully selected men, specially trained to lead assaults. Opinions differed as to the use of this system, but I personally thought it a bad one, for it meant, as it were, skimming the cream from the milk of the German battalions, just at the time when their morale was beginning to decline.

When I went forward, I found myself in the middle of a free-for-all fight. The flanks of the division had remained firm, but in the centre the *Sturm Truppen* had captured our front line and a part of the support line. In one place they had advanced even further to where some men were digging a dugout that was to have been advanced brigade headquarters for the coming attack. An improvised counter attack had cleared them out of this, but they had taken away the digging party as prisoners. Had our troops been experienced, they would probably have been able to halt the *Sturm Truppen* from the start, but it must be remembered that most of our infantry were inexperienced boys fresh from England during this action.

I found that my Stokes gunners had not done too badly. One gun and considerable stores of ammunition had had to be left behind in the old front line, but our casualties only amounted to a few wounded, and the gun teams had taken up new positions and were beginning to get into action again. One corporal had behaved with great good sense in this, his first action. He had withdrawn with his gun and team to a spot slightly behind the new front line, dug in and even rustled up a sizeable stock of shells. He had sited the gun with some skill, for I found that he enjoyed an excellent view of the communication trench between our old front and support lines, of which, at this point the former was held by the Germans, and the latter by our infantry. I found him absolutely furious with frustration!

"I got all this fixed, Sir," he said "and I had just begun firing when one of the infantry officers came down here and ordered me to stop, said we would draw the enemy's fire, just look at that trench now, Sir."

I looked at the communication trench in which our infantry had thrown up an improvised block about 300 yards from where we were. On our side of the block I could dimly see the movement of some of our men; on the other side I could clearly see the tops of the helmets of the sizeable party of Boches advancing gingerly up the trench towards the block. "I think we can forget about that infantry officer," I said. "He is new here, but in this division we have always been taught to kill Germans, particularly when they are asking for it. Twenty rounds rapid fire." The delighted corporal and his gun team waited to hear no more. A shower of Stokes shells burst in and round the communication trench and we had the satisfaction of seeing the long row of German helmets turning and moving off, considerably faster than before, in the opposite direction.

Had our infantry on our side of the block realised what was going on, they could have chased out the disgruntled Germans, affected a killing and, probably, recaptured this part of our old front line without difficulty. But these raw troops, belonging, incidentally, to another brigade, lacked the initiative to take the opportunity that my gun teams had been able to provide for them on the spur of the moment and did not move and were too far off for me to be able to communicate with them. Even had this been possible in time, whoever was in charge of them did not seem to be spoiling for a fight, and would probably have ignored a communication from an officer unknown to him, belonging to another brigade. I waited for some time to see whether the Germans would make another attempt, but nothing happened and I went on my way, leaving with the corporal a note stating that he was acting under my orders, and that I would be responsible for his actions.

A short distance to the rear I noticed a small flag outside a dugout indicating that it was the headquarters of one of the battalions in the 55th Brigade, and called in to see their lieutenant-colonel, whom I knew, officially, quite well, although our dealings had, hitherto, been on a formal basis, and he was not a personal friend of mine. I knew him to be a most capable lieutenant-colonel, and a brave man with a well-earned D.S.O. and M.C., so I was surprised to find him lying in a bunk. He was probably ill, he certainly looked exhausted. He told me that with the situation continually changing, his new company commanders had not been giving him adequate information reports, and he was nearly in the dark as to what his battalion was doing. I was able to give him a fairly accurate account of the situation as I saw it. He seemed genuinely grateful, thanked me earnestly for having done him a good turn, and said he would not forget it. I was rather mystified by this, but continued on my way back to my headquarters, and forgot all about it.

I had got some distance along the trench when, without warning, the German artillery put down an extremely heavy bombardment all around the spot where I was. One 77mm shell whistled so close over my head that it seemed to touch me, and burst in the next traverse of the trench.

Captain Philip Heath

When Private Apted and I got round the corner, we saw a terrible sight: the body of a young officer,[1] practically decapitated by the shell that missed us, was lying at the bottom of the trench in a great pool of blood. He was a boy, fresh from England, whom I knew, although not as well as I would have liked to, owing to my return from the infantry to trench mortar work. Although he had only been out such a short time, he had already become one of the best-liked officers in the battalion, owing to his gaiety and great sense of humour. There had been one awkward occasion, which had been a source of merriment throughout the brigade. One day, when his battalion was on platoon training, the lieutenant-colonel had walked behind a haystack and found this boy performing feats of juggling with three live Mills bombs for the benefit of his delighted platoon. We picked up the body, placed it under cover as best we could, and bolted for our lives to get out of the shelled area.

To make matters worse, the trench came abruptly to an end for, owing to the German attack, we were in an area where the trenches had not been properly laid out, and we found that the only way for us to get back was out of the trench and over the open through a formidable belt of barbed wire. Somehow we managed to struggle through this with the German shells bursting all round us, and finally ran for dear life until we had emerged from the barrage area into comparative safety. It was one of the narrowest escapes I ever had, and it seemed a miracle to us both that neither of us had been hit.

---

1   Second-Lieutenant Douglas Stevens, attached 7th Buffs. Killed in action 6 August 1918. Buried at Beacon Cemetery, Sailly-Laurette.

In preparation for the coming battle, Brigadier-General Wood had established advanced brigade headquarters close to my own dugout and on my arrival there was a message that he wanted to see me immediately. I went over, just as I was, and found the brigadier-general seated at a table in a large dugout. I managed to go through the motions of a salute, and then found that I could not speak. I must have presented a revolting spectacle. Owing to the excitements of the morning I had not washed or shaved. My uniform was badly torn by my struggle in the barbed wire and covered in the blood of that poor boy, and my puttees were lying in festoons round my ankles. There I stood, struggling for speech, with my body trembling. I felt that I was just about out of control, and might burst into tears, or go crazy.

The brigadier-general handled the situation superbly. He looked at me thoughtfully, and said very quietly and gently: "Heath, you are not properly dressed. Your puttees are coming down, go and tidy up a bit and then come back here." It was absolutely typical of him. With his amazing natural knowledge of the psychology of soldiers, he had said exactly what was necessary to make me pull myself together, without the slightest anger or bullying. I loved him that day and never lost a great affection for him, for he had given me back something that, without realising it, I had valued enormously, my own self-respect. I even found myself laughing genuinely, not hysterically. It was so exactly like him to select my puttees for criticism. After a quarter of an hour's ministrations at the hands of my servant Wade, I returned, comparatively presentable, to the brigadier-general and was able to give him a coherent report as to the situation in the lines.

It was finally decided that next morning, 7 August, a local attack would be carried out in order to recapture our old front and support lines. This would be considered by the Germans as a normal reaction on our part, and they would probably be expecting something of the sort. If we made use of all the resources at our disposal, the new artillery already in position, and the tanks already hidden nearby for use in the big battle, this local operation would have been child's play, for the Germans could not have had time to turn round the defence positions in their newly captured trenches and would be blown out of them by our great artillery concentration. However, it would be fatal to do this, for it would give the whole game away for the attack being planned for 8 August.

On the morning of the 7 August our local counter attack took place, to the accompaniment of a brisk barrage carried out by about a quarter of our artillery strength. Although not wholly successful, it was a creditable achievement for our untried men. The whole of the old support line was recaptured, and the 8th East Surreys succeeded in seizing and holding a part of the old front line. The *Sturm Truppen* had been relieved the previous night, and the new German defenders were not a very distinguished lot. Shortly after the 8th East Surreys' attack, I went up to join them, and was very pleased with what I found in the front line. I found a Stokes gun that had been left behind in the attack of 6 August. It was in good condition, as was the shell dump close by, and we soon went into action. But this was not all, for the Germans had obligingly brought up, and left behind, one of their own *Leicht Minenwerfer* (light trench mortars), the opposite number of the Stokes gun, together with a stock of shells. It had a heavy base, from which projected a solid steel cylinder, of which the angle could be raised or lowered according to the range of the target. The *Leicht Minenwerfer* had a much slower rate of fire than the Stokes, but was more accurate and had a considerably longer range.

Our line was under vigorous fire from a German machine gun, in enfilade from the north, and well out of range of the Stokes gun. I had never seen one of these *Leicht Minenwerfer* before, but it seemed easy enough to fire, as, indeed, it proved to be. It appeared to be the very weapon to silence the German machine gun. We let fly, rather gingerly, with a couple of trial rounds which went satisfactorily in the required direction, and, after adjusting for range, really got down to business, delivering a steady stream of "pineapples" on the unfortunate German machine gunners. I don't know whether we succeeded in hitting them, but we obtained the results that we needed, for the machine gun abruptly ceased fire, and caused no more trouble. Artillery fire continued throughout the day, and the Germans made a few half-hearted attempts to counter attack without success. In the evening our troops that had taken part in the action were relieved, and were not concerned with the great assault of the following day, 8 August, as had previously been planned. Their place was taken by battalions of 53rd Brigade, together with our 7th Queens, which had been in reserve during 6 and 7 August.

The battle of 8 August was, perhaps, the most complete and brilliant victory ever gained up to that time by the British Army. General Erich Ludendorff called 8 August the "black day" of the German army. The Germans had had no idea of the coming assault and were taken completely by surprise. It was a misty morning. At dawn, 450 tanks, preceded by a great artillery barrage fired by more than 2000 guns, advanced to the attack on a wide front, with the infantry of the Fourth Army behind them to consolidate. All objectives, some four or five miles away, were captured, and more than 11,000 prisoners were taken, at very small cost to ourselves. It was in this battle that Lieutenant-Colonel Christopher Bushell V.C.,[1] 7th Queen's, was fatally wounded whilst directing tanks and urging his men forward.

Our division, on the extreme left of the line of attack, acted as a hinge to the whole movement, so that its objectives were limited and were reached with little difficulty. One of the 7th West Kents' company commanders, an old friend of mine named Captain Albert Macdonald, after reaching his objective, could not resist the temptation to explore the situation in front of him, and, after informing his O.C. of his intentions, set off into the blue with his men. After a mile or two, they suddenly came upon a German heavy battery at the moment when its unsuspecting commander was strolling across to his officers' mess for breakfast. To his indignation, he and his men were lined up and marched back without breakfast to our prisoners' cages. Macdonald and his men

---

1   Lieutenant-Colonel Christopher Bushell V.C., D.S.O. Killed in action 8 August 1918. Buried at Querrieu British Cemetery.

went happily on right beyond the battle zone and had covered about five miles when a message arrived from headquarters ordering him to return. He then discovered that, in the woods on either side of his position, there were large concentrations of Germans preparing to move up into the battle. The company was soon spotted and had a spirited game of hide and seek with the Germans, moving back in Indian file and concealing themselves in the corn. They eventually arrived back in our lines after an exciting day out.

As a result of this great battle the Germans began to pull out eastwards all along the line. They tried to move slowly and deliberately, in order to save their artillery and stores, and it was by no means easy for our forces to hustle them owing to difficulties of transport over the wilderness of the old battlefields. The Germans were still holding Albert, and, after a few days' rest, our division moved back into the position it had previously held in front of the little town. During this short interlude I was out, one day, with my 55th Trench Mortar Battery when we met Brigadier-General Wood. He called me aside and informed me that I was to leave command of the battery forthwith, as he wanted me at brigade headquarters as assistant brigade major and intelligence officer. I was delighted at this entirely unexpected news.

I had felt for some time that I had spent too long in the front line and could not stand much more of it. I could still face danger, but it was becoming more and more of an effort. Previously I had often been terrified, like all fighting soldiers, but, knowing the necessity of mastering and concealing my fear, had usually, I hoped, been able to do so. But now I found that I had to force myself to leave the shelter of a dugout if shelling was taking place. My deepest private fear was that I might unexpectedly disgrace myself, and endanger the men I commanded, by breaking down or losing my head.

To me, life at brigade headquarters would seem like paradise; a proper comfortable night's rest, no more men's lives and training to worry about. As for danger, knowing the brigadier-general's disposition, I was certain of never having a dull moment while accompanying him into battle, but, although it might be crazy, it would be fun compared to the dreary, never-ending shell dodging that I had been doing for the last three years. Leaving the battery meant very little to me now. It had become a fairly efficient unit again. But, the new officers and men were strangers to me and I cared little for them, whereas, in the old days, I had the feeling, which I believe was shared by the others, that we were a band of brothers so that every death in action of a man became a personal loss to us all. On the other hand, the officers in the brigade staff were all good friends of mine, with whom I should be happy to live and work.

The brigadier-general's decision was typical of the man himself; kindly, unconventional, and full of good sense. My recent deplorable appearance before him, with my puttees falling down, had evidently not been held against me, and with his talent for getting the best out of those under him, he had probably realised that my battery might suffer if I was kept in charge of it too long, while it was his duty to see that it was in the highest state of efficiency. Yet, I could still be useful doing other work. The unconventionality of the decision lay in the fact that, according to army regulations, my new post was officially non-existent, for there was no provision made in army establishment for someone to assist the brigade major. The same was true of the post of intelligence officer. However, I knew that the brigadier-general, with his superb capacity for ignoring red tape, would take care of this problem. In fact he accomplished this so successfully that divisional headquarters, who could easily have returned me to duty with the battery, not only made no objections, but actually called me, later on, to work on a special job, which lasted for three weeks, at their own headquarters.

The fact of the matter was that I had become a unique case, almost a freak. There were several officers who had come out to France with the division, still serving with it in an undamaged condition, but these were all engaged on staff or special technical work. There were officers of the original division still doing front-line work, but these had been wounded, some several times, and had had long spells of rest at home. My case was different for I was one of the original officers of the division, had served with it almost uninterruptedly doing front line work, and had achieved the feat of retaining a whole skin. There was probably no other officer in the division with a similar record. Anyone with experience of front-line work in France and Flanders will agree that to serve over three years in this way, without a wound to show for it, constituted a near miracle. Moreover, I was, by this time, fairly well known to most of the senior officers of the division and, in all probability, it had simply been decided that I had done as much as could be expected, and was due for an easier and safer job, in spite of red tape.

The brigadier-general's decision was also sensible, I think, from his own point of view. With his propensity for getting mixed up in battles, somebody had to look after things at brigade headquarters, and this would, normally, be the brigade major. On the other hand, it was highly desirable that, on these occasions, the brigadier-general should be accompanied by an experienced officer, well known to the rest of the brigade, to act as liaison between him and the units under his command. Naturally, there were plenty of other jobs to do as well in the fighting that was to come. It seemed to me that my appointment had genuinely served a useful purpose. From this time until the Armistice on 11 November 1918 I had what amounted to a roving commission in the fighting. The brigadier-general, if on the rampage, would be accompanied by Major Randolph Chell, the brigade major, or myself. If during an engagement he did not need me, he would sometimes send me up the line on my own, to do what I could to help. It was surprising how often opportunities arose to give needed information, or even once or twice take charge of some leaderless body of men and show them how to get on with the war.

About this time an army order appeared from which I learned that I had been awarded a bar to the Military Cross. The citation read:

"For conspicuous gallantry and good leadership when commanding a trench-mortar battery. By skilful handling of his guns he was of great assistance to the officer commanding the forward area in helping to establish the battalion on position; and he also brought into action three enemy light trench mortars and inflicted losses, besides silencing an enemy machine gun. He behaved with great gallantry and energy throughout."

I derived no satisfaction from this award. In the first place, as far as I could see, I had done nothing in particular to deserve it. It was the general opinion among army officers in the line at this time that the M.C. was no longer worth having, for the powers who controlled their distribution had begun to hand them out in large numbers to officers whose conduct, however admirable, could by no possible stretch of imagination be described as gallant, for the very simple reason that they had never been in action in their lives.

In the 18th (Eastern) Division there was an unofficial award. This was a certificate on parchment, signed by the divisional commander, thanking and congratulating the recipient for his good work and devotion to duty. These certificates were greatly valued by the men who sent them home to their wives and sweethearts, thereby gaining a good deal of prestige. A document of this kind was tangible proof that its owner was a good soldier, for it was signed by someone who knew what he was talking about. These certificates were given to other ranks only, not for specific acts of gallantry but steady service, and duty well done in the front line.

XII

Road to Victory

August–November 1918

The division lay facing Albert and took part in a general attack on 24 August. A big concentration of artillery had been prepared, but, as things turned out, it was far more powerful than was really necessary. On the previous night, an 8th East Surreys patrol discovered that one of the River Ancre bridges had been left unguarded, and the bridgehead was promptly occupied. This enabled the East Surreys, at dawn next day, to storm the little town, and force their way up Tara Hill on the eastern side, with their flanks fully secured. I, myself, had a roving commission on this day, and spent most of it on Tara Hill, acting as liaison between the various units, whenever I could be of use.

For the first time in my life, I was watching Open Warfare. It was fascinating to see units advancing by section rushes, the officers conveying their commands by whistle and hand signals. German opposition was poor, and, towards the end of the afternoon, we had taken Tara Hill and our other objectives with moderate casualties.

The only thing to spoil the day was gas, my first really serious experience of this horrible weapon. Albert was full of mustard gas, and one had the impression that, through the entire day, the German artillery was firing nothing but gas shells. The troops were all supplied with excellent gas masks, which had one key disadvantage: while wearing them it was very difficult to advance more than a few yards, a fact that apparently had never been foreseen, however obvious it was to anyone that attempted to do so.

Any sceptic can prove this problem to his own satisfaction. All that is necessary is to pick a suitable route over three miles, mostly uphill, and, on as warm a day as possible, carrying some 30 pounds on your back, with a clothes peg on your nose, set off to complete the course as quickly as possible, then see what happens. That is a fair description of what we were supposed to do, except that we stood an excellent chance of death by asphyxiation if the gas mask was removed. The mask completely covered the head. A clip went over the nose and one breathed through a sort of hollow mouth piece attached to a tube and a valve that caused all the inhaled air to pass through a tin containing chemicals, which purified it.

Finding it impossible to advance in the masks, we were faced with two alternatives. These were either to pass the afternoon in them, sitting on Tara Hill, which seemed unattractive, or take them off and hope for the best, and that, in fact, was what we did. The short-term results of this decision were excellent. The objectives were reached and very few men appeared to be affected. As to the long-term effects, I am not so sure. Many went down with heavy colds and coughs in the ensuing days, and I myself have suffered from bronchial trouble ever since I left the army, but it is impossible to be certain that this gas was the cause.

From 8 August, the war had been turned into a kind of running fight, which, I imagine, the Germans enjoyed considerably less than we did. As a result of that great battle, it must have been obvious to every German soldier on the Western Front that the game was up, and that there was no future in it. One would have thought that the German leaders might have had the sense, if not the humanity, to realise that the sooner they threw in their hand, the better it would be for the Fatherland. Instead of doing so, they attempted to retreat in good order, pausing to fight whenever a good terrain became available. Possibly they hoped that they could retire, maybe as far as the Rhine, and then hold on until they could obtain suitable terms from the Allies.

Marshal Ferdinand Foch, the commander-in-chief of the Allied Armies, had other ideas. The German retirement with guns and stores became too slow, and Foch gave them no rest. In every attack a time comes when the infantry outstrips its artillery and supplies, and the momentum is lost. This is, of course, the most favourable moment to launch a counter attack. But these assaults, although launched on fairly large fronts, were limited. An attack would be launched, the Germans would send up their reserves for the counter attack and then Foch would start another attack somewhere else. As this process continued, the German troops, more and more bewildered and discouraged, began to surrender *en masse* until, on 11 November, General Erich Ludendorff threw in his hand altogether. This will explain the kind of fighting from now on, and show why we began to capture, with slight losses, some of the strongholds which in 1916 had caused the loss of thousands of our men.

From Tara Hill we moved on through Happy Valley, Carnoy and Montauban, the village that we had taken in our first great fight on 1 July 1916. The first real resistance was encountered when we reached the ruins of Combles, which had been the scene of heavy fighting during the Somme offensive of 1916. This time we took the village with the loss of a few hundred men in an action, which was part of a general assault. I was again acting in a freelance capacity and it was a truly fascinating experience. For the first time I was to learn that the phrase "the science of war" could have a real meaning, and, from a ringside seat, see what happened when a clever general met a stupid one.

At dawn, with no artillery preparatory bombardment, but with the infantry following a rolling barrage, Major-General Sir Richard Lee, commanding the 18th (Eastern) Division, opened the assault on a one-battalion front, on the right of the line. Here the Germans held Priez Farm on high ground, the key to whole position. Two companies of the 8th East Surreys led by Captain Frederick Gaywood, my old second in command, and carrying nothing but rifles and bombs, rushed the farm going hell for leather, and had captured it before the Germans knew what had happened. On the left of Gaywood's force, the remainder of the battalion moved forward, not in a straight line with them, but so as to create a curve. If we had acted according to the methods used up to now, one of two things would have occurred: we might have sat down and awaited a counter attack; alternately, using fresh troops, a further advance would have been attempted in the same direction as the first one. Accordingly, the German general began to send up troops into the trench line facing the East Surreys. When our second attack was launched, it came from the battalion on the left of the East Surreys, not in the direction of the first attack, but spreading towards the left so as to increase the arc. The East Surreys stayed where they were. The Germans, seeing this, began to alter the direction of their own reinforcements towards the new attack, which afforded an excellent opportunity for target practice to the East Surreys. Our position could be compared to an open sack with the enemy hastening into its neck, which was slowly narrowing. A third attack took place, still to the left of the first two, still edging to the left. As the process continued, the bewildered Germans soon began to wonder whether they were coming or going.

I arrived at Priez Farm not long after its capture and, with little risk, could see exactly what was going on. Little groups of Germans would appear, keeping low and moving in military formation. They would be greeted with a volley of rifle fire from the delighted East Surreys' boys on their flank, mostly newcomers taking part in their first fight. To my surprise and pleasure, some of them began to show signs of fighting madness, the old "lust of battle." Quite close to us we could see a large group of Germans, discouraged by the rifle fire, lying on their bellies, their packs sticking up. The East Surreys were firing at them for all they were worth, and I actually saw some of them fix bayonets and, without orders to, climb out of their trench to finish off the enemy. It was extremely rare to find men starting on a bayonet charge of their own volition. I and some East Surreys' officers and non-commissioned officers actually had to haul them back into the trench by their boots, explaining that what they wanted to do would ruin the whole party, for the Germans would then see what was really going on and stop sending their troops into the trap.

Then came the moment when that cunning old spider, Major-General Lee, decided that he had the Germans exactly where he wanted them. One last dash and all the Germans in front of the division were completely encircled. The rest of the afternoon was spent in compelling their surrender. In a way, I began to feel rather sorry for them; they had fought quite bravely, and what had happened was not their fault. It was splendid to see that our old major-general, if only allowed to use his brains, could make his opposite number over the way, with all his years of German-army training, look like a bungling amateur. Even this was not the end. Lee still had one fresh battalion up his sleeve, and late in the afternoon he let them loose. I saw them set off, pursuing the demoralised Germans (those who had been stopped in time from entering the trap), all hell for leather. As far as we were concerned it was a complete break through, a truly glorious experience for the attackers.

That evening we had just begun supper in the brigade mess, when the brigade major was called out to deal with a problem. Two infantrymen were there in charge of a party of some 50 prisoners. They had been ordered to take their charges as far as brigade headquarters and then return to the line. We had no men available to take the Germans on to the divisional cage for prisoners, so the problem was what were we to do with them? Various solutions were proposed by us all. Brigadier-General Edward Wood looked up from his plate of curry and remarked to no one in particular: "Take away their boots!" We all stopped talking in astonishment, and there was a roar of laughter at this novel solution. "What are you all laughing at?" enquired the brigadier-general. "That is what we used to do in South Africa." So, the Germans were temporarily deprived of their boots and spent the night in a dugout and the brigade guard was told to keep an eye on the dugout entrance as part of his duties. Even the prisoners were grinning as they shambled down the dugout steps in their socks. They gave no trouble.

The next stand made by the Germans was in front of the village of Ronssoy. It was a strong position and in 1917 it had been one of the principal outposts of the Hindenburg line. A set-piece, large-scale battle was planned to deal with the whole position. On the appointed day, after an early breakfast of curry, the brigadier-general and I mounted our horses and set off towards the battle. He was a great man for curry. During his early days with our brigade he had spent much time instructing the cook how to prepare it *á la mode de Poona*. At first this witch's brew nearly blew our heads off, but after a time I got to like it and, although the idea horrified me at first, I used to join the brigadier-general in his barbarous habit of breakfasting on it.

Hitherto I have made no mention of my horse, Molly. She was one of the most attractive horses I have known, and I was very fond of her. She was a bay mare, in reality too small for my six-feet-and-two-inch height, but she made up for it with a great heart, and a very long trotting stride, lifting her forelegs like a trotting racehorse. Although I knew nothing of her pedigree, I was sure that there was good blood in her. On the first day that I rode her, she had thrown up her head and bolted. I had no control whatsoever, and began to wonder what would happen next, as she was galloping as hard as she could go towards a sunken lane with a drop of well over five feet. When we got to the lane, instead of blundering, thereby causing both of us to break our necks, she collected herself and jumped, making a perfect landing so that I never even fell off. Luckily the lane led uphill and I at least managed to pull her up. I at once had her fitted with a martingale and had no more trouble with her.

In many ways horses resemble people in their qualities and vices, and Molly had many of the attributes of a high-spirited, well-bred girl that was full of mischief but utterly without vice. She was extremely intelligent. Whenever we were out of the line, I used to visit the horse lines to see that she was comfortable. She would whinny when she heard me coming, and would nuzzle round my pockets to find the apple she considered her due. She made such a fuss when she couldn't find it, but at last I would produce one from a hidden pocket, and we made it up. Her courage was superb. Once I had to ride her 35 miles in a day and she tried to bolt over the last mile. Another time we were at full gallop on some downs when she suddenly jumped about two feet into the air and went on her way. I went back to see if anything was wrong and found a field-telephone wire a foot above the ground left by some signaller. On several occasions we ran into shellfire together and she ignored it completely. The only thing she would not put up with were brass bands. The noise made her almost uncontrollable, and she would remain upset and trembling for the rest of the day. The men were very fond of her, and some of them told me what happened when, just before the Armistice, I had to return her to duty with the battery. Evidently she did not approve of my successor. The first time he rode her, she decided, after half a mile of weary progress, that enough was enough. She turned about, galloped back, neatly tipped off her rider at the entrance to the farm where she was stabled and briskly went into her stall.

Anyhow, on this morning before Ronssoy, the brigadier-general and I went on our way, talking of this and that, and passed through the ruins of the small village of St. Emilie. As we moved down the road, the artillery fire was steadily increasing, and we soon heard the rattle of German machineguns extremely close to us. I began to feel a little apprehensive. I would certainly not have put it past the brigadier-general to have decided that it would be a nice change to lead his brigade on horseback. What is more, I really believe I would have gone along with him with the utmost pleasure, if he had tried it. On the other hand, I knew that map reading was not his strong point, and that, quite possibly, he had not the remotest notion as to where he was. Still, it was not for me to say anything. As we passed the ruins of a group of houses, amid a terrific racket of shellfire and machine guns, the brigadier-general remarked:

"This is St. Emilie, isn't it, Heath?"

"No, Sir," I replied, trying to keep a stiff upper lip, "it's Ronssoy."

Where we were taking our morning ride had been in German hands only a few minutes before, and the fighting was still going on a few hundred yards away on the other side of the village. "Oh, is it?" the brigadier-general replied. He told me to return to brigade headquarters with instructions that he wanted to give to Major Randolph Chell, the brigade major. "I am going to have a look round," he said. Then he dismounted slowly, handed over his horse to his groom and, grasping his enormous lance and pennon, away he stalked into the battle quite alone.

At this moment a large shrapnel shell burst in the air just over me, showering fragments of metal in all directions. Neither Molly nor I was hurt. Molly, like the brave little lady that she was, quietly ignored the shrapnel. I soon turned her round and had her galloping through the barrage back to brigade headquarters. I returned to the battle in the afternoon. I was unable to locate the brigadier-general, but several people had met him trudging about and said that he had refused all offers of an escort. The attack proceeded successfully, and at the end of the day we were on our final objective with another big haul of prisoners.

As far as I was concerned, only one noteworthy incident took place. I was lying in a ditch, well up with the infantry, talking to the team of one of my Stokes guns, when I noticed a large German plane flying very low, up and down our line, evidently on reconnaissance. Our machine guns were firing at it, without apparent success, and the remarkably brave German pilot continued to fly up and down, without paying any attention to them. A Stokes gun was about the most unsuitable weapon possible for such a target, because, at this stage of the war, all the shells were fitted with percussion fuses. That meant that nothing but a direct hit in mid-air could have the slightest effect. To obtain one with a slow moving shell like the Stokes on a target moving at about 100 miles an hour would have been nothing less than a miracle. However, miracles do sometimes occur, and, as the plane was flying just in front of our line, any shells that I fired would do no harm to our troops, and might even damage the Germans. I took the gun myself and, when the plane came down the line again, fired 10 rounds at full speed. I missed, but one of the shells seemed to be going straight for the plane. Afterwards the men swore that it could not have passed more than ten feet from it, and I think they were right. At all events, it made off and we did not see it again. Had I succeeded in hitting it, it would have been almost a unique feat for a Stokes gun. It was rumoured that it had been accomplished once, but I never heard it confirmed.

That evening, Brigadier-General Wood turned up safe at brigade headquarters, having clearly had a most enjoyable day out. As he stalked up the trenches, soon after leaving me, he had heard talking coming from a dugout. He armed himself with rocks which he hurled down the entrance – and out bolted eight Germans who must have been astonished to find that they had surrendered to an unarmed brigadier-general. The latter marched them down the trench, handed them over to an escort and went on his way. He had carried out a reconnaissance by himself in front of our positions. He had given some extremely sensible orders, holding back an attack that was due to start, because it was not the right moment. The brigadier-general led it himself successfully when he considered the right moment had arrived. He also had two bullet holes through his tin hat, but he didn't know how that had happened. We were relieved from the line next day, which was no more than our due after nearly two months continuous fighting. I then went on leave.

I returned from leave to France to find the 18th (Eastern) Division just coming back from the line. At this time I was ordered to divisional headquarters for three weeks, as a replacement for an officer who was away. I was not comfortable there and was thankful to be able to return to brigade headquarters when my time was up. It was not that I felt that there was anything wrong with the divisional staff, on the contrary, most of them were doing their jobs extremely well. It was simply that I and they came from different worlds and did not speak the same language. In particular, the divisional commander, Major-General Lee, was a complete enigma to me for I had never met anyone who was remotely akin to him. As a master map reader and tactician there can have been very few to equal him in the whole of the British army, but in all the other great problems of war, he seemed not to take the slightest interest.

I knew already, of course, that throughout the division Major-General Lee was nothing but a name to be obeyed. But here, in his own headquarters,

Captain Philip Heath

he seemed to be a completely negative personality, and that he wanted it to be that way. He was always courteous, he never bullied, or swore or lost his temper nor, apparently, did he have any desire to have friends. During meals he was silent. The rest of the day he would spend shut in his office studying maps, moving his little paper flags about on them, receiving messages and issuing orders, all without the slightest interest in the men whose lives he was manipulating. One night the message came through of the surrender of Bulgaria, the first of Germany's allies to throw up the sponge. I took the message to him, feeling very pleased and hoping that he, too, would show some human sign of pleasure. He looked at me, said "Oh?" and went on with his work. It was easy to respect a man of his talents, but, for me at any rate, genuine liking was out of the question.

Of all the divisional staff, I found the G.S.O.1. (General Staff Officer, Grade 1) Lieutenant-Colonel Guy Blewitt by far the most likeable. The G.S.O.1. is responsible under the divisional commander for all operational matters. Blewitt knew that I had a sound knowledge of three foreign languages. One day he told me that the Intelligence Corps was looking for recruits, and he had mentioned my name at G.H.Q. as being very suitable for this work. He was going next day to G.H.Q. and, if I liked, I could accompany him for an interview. I gladly accepted the suggestion. Apart from the fact that I felt I had done my full share of front line work, I had already done a little unofficial intelligence work, by interviewing the occasional prisoners, translating captured documents and so on. I felt that it was a type of work in which I could be of real use.

The next day, Blewitt and I motored to Montreuil where we arrived in time for lunch. I was taken into an enormous mess room full of junior staff officers. Everyone was most polite, and I detested the whole atmosphere. From everything that these young officers said, it was absolutely clear that they had never been near the front, that they never intended to go near it, and that they considered that anyone who did not agree must obviously be out of his mind. From their point of view, they were quite right, but I did not see how I could possibly live, let alone work, in such an atmosphere.

After lunch I went off for my interview with a colonel of the Intelligence Corps. He was a charming, elderly man who did his best to make me feel at ease. He tried out my languages. We spoke German together for five minutes, and he told me that I spoke it better than he did. Then there was a test of my French including a written translation from English into French. The colonel remarked that my French accent, although not as perfect as my German accent, was also extremely good and that my general knowledge of the languages was most satisfactory. I told him that I thought that my knowledge of Italian was about equal to my French, to which the colonel replied that he was quite willing to take my word for it, as he had no knowledge himself of Italian.

The colonel said I was the very type of young officer that the Intelligence Corps was looking for. He would just take down a few particulars: full name, age, surname of my father's parents and mother's maiden name. To the latter question, I replied that her maiden name was Schmidt, to which the colonel replied that in that case I was not a suitable candidate for the Intelligence

Corps and that he could not make use of my services. He asked no more questions. I replied politely that if the Intelligence Corps considered I could not be trusted because of my mother's maiden name, for which neither she nor I were responsible, it seemed odd that for three years I had been not only allowed, but ordered to be in front line positions, (for which, incidentally, I had been awarded an M.C. and Bar) from which I could have crossed over to the German positions on any night that suited me, carrying full details of everything that was going on in my division, and probably a good deal more. The colonel replied that he was acting under orders that he had not made, and that personally he much regretted that he could not make use of my services. Back I went to divisional headquarters with Lieutenant-Colonel Blewitt, heartily thankful that I should not have to work in an organisation run on such incredibly foolish principles, in such a completely uncongenial atmosphere. Thus ended my one and only experience of life at G.H.Q. It was, however, enough to enable me to begin to understand the utter lack of comprehension that existed between the High Command and the fighting troops, the key to all our losses and setbacks.

Soon after returning to 55th Brigade headquarters, I had one more outing into battle with Brigadier-General Wood. It was a comparatively mild affair, although the brigadier-general, as ever, acted true to form. The position was in front of a village called Bousies, not far from Le Cateau, and the German resistance was steadily weakening. The divisional assault was to start at dawn, and the brigadier-general insisted on going up to see what was going on, in spite of the fact that his brigade was in reserve and would take no part in the initial action. We rose very early and had arrived at the lines of the field guns. The gunners all busily preparing for the rolling barrage due to open some 10 minutes later. In the semi darkness the brigadier-general noticed an elderly artillery officer giving instructions: "Why," exclaimed Wood, "if it isn't my old friend, Bill!" We went across and the two old men nearly fell into one another's arms in their pleasure at this unexpected meeting. There they stood, in the deathly quiet before Zero, chatting away about their service together in India where they had been brother officers.

Suddenly, at Zero hour, all our guns opened fire together. Amid the uproar the two old brigadier-generals went on talking away about Poona and Hyderabad, without taking the slightest notice of the din, while I stood there slightly apprehensive, knowing full well that it was only a question of a few minutes before the German counter-battery barrage descended on us. Sure enough, down it came just as Brigadier-General Wood was offering his flask to the other brigadier-general. For all the notice they took of the German shells falling around them they might have been swapping yarns over a whisky and soda at the United Services Club. At last, the gunners' brigadier-general remembered his duties. They parted warmly and Brigadier-General Wood strolled back with me to the curry breakfast awaiting him at brigade headquarters.

Three days later, Brigadier-General Wood had a severe rheumatic attack and had to be evacuated to England. I saw him off to the station, and nearly broke down at our parting. It was like losing one's father, for that is how he had treated me from the start, and I should have been proud to have had a father like him. I lived abroad for eight years after the war, so that I was only able to see the brigadier-general two or three more times, while I was visiting England. Each time he was as warm hearted and kind as ever, but I felt that he was not doing well and was not happy. I heard for certain that his financial situation was becoming poor, and there were rumours, unconfirmed, that he had been caught unawares by some of the more unscrupulous traders, operating at that time in the jungle of the City. At any rate he died in 1929, soon after my return to London, and I was able to attend his funeral. There is no need to say more about him, except that I held him in the highest esteem and affection, and shall never forget him.

Lieutenant-Colonel Alfred Irwin took temporary command of the 55th Brigade, which went into battle for the last time on 6 November 1918, one of the unforgettable days of my life. The 18th (Eastern) Division's objective was, with another division on its flank, to capture the whole of the great Forest of Mormal near Le Cateau, the town where the British Expeditionary Force had begun the fighting in 1914. The forest could have proved a formidable obstacle for our forces. But by this time the Germans were on the run, and much of the wood had been cut down by them, so that it was not difficult to penetrate, and we were confident of achieving the capture without too much difficulty. The forest had probably been used for hunting before the war, and several straight narrow rides had been cut through the trees, whose surfaces in the wet autumn weather were most slippery. The plan of attack was extremely simple. The 53rd and 54th Brigades were to open the attack at dawn, while our brigade was in reserve about a mile from the forest and was to leap-frog through at 10.30 a.m. and advance until it reached the final objective. At this point, if all went well, the division would be "squeezed out" by the divisions on either flank and would retire from the battle.

Everything went exactly according to plan. At 10.30 a.m. I was at advanced brigade headquarters talking to Irwin when two monsters appeared, the like of which I had never seen before. They were armoured cars, under command of Fourth Army headquarters. They had been sent up, entirely without previous warning, to lend a hand. The crews of these two cars seemed a tough, hard-bitten lot. For the little subaltern in command of them, this was his first engagement. Although very young, he seemed an excellent type for the job: cheerful, sensible and competent. He and I made friends at once, and he was soon briefly explaining to me the marvels that were contained in his two armoured cars.

Irwin strolled over to us: "Now would you like to go in the other car, P.G.?" he said to me, smiling. "Nothing in the world I should like more, Sir," I replied. Irwin turned to the little subaltern, whose name I have forgotten, but who will hence forward be referred to as Smith. "Now, young man," he said, "You are under my orders for this operation only, and I don't want to interfere in your command in other ways, but I think Captain Heath should be in charge of this expedition. You are an expert in armoured cars, but Heath is senior to you and probably knows a good deal more about the ways of Germans than you do." He looked at us both, his eyes twinkling. "Somehow," he said, "I don't see you two boys quarrelling about procedure." Smith beamed: "Of course, Sir," he said, "It's quite understood." Irwin said: "All right, off you go. You know the final objective, I can't give you orders about what I don't know. Use your common sense, kill as many Huns as you can, and look after yourselves."

Off we went, I in the leading car, down narrow lanes towards the forest. The first hour or so was far from what I had anticipated for, in an endeavour to slow up our advance, the Germans had rolled great tree trunks and anything else they could find across the road, and, every time, we had to stop to remove them. The cars contained ropes, axes and all sorts of equipment for such a purpose, but it was a maddeningly slow process and I began to think we should miss the battle altogether. As we were working at one of the blocks, an enormous English tank, which we had not heard owing to the noise of the artillery fire, heaved its way over the hedge and crashed down into the sunken road, almost on top of us. Luckily its commander spotted in time that we were friendly and did not open fire.

As we were tackling yet another block, a shell from a German heavy artillery gun burst on top of a nearby cottage. We heard moans, and rescued from the ruins an old couple who had been asleep on the first floor and had been blown out of bed into the wreckage on the ground floor. They were unhurt, and the old man's language about the Germans was formidable. All this took time, but at least we got away, the old people blessing us and adjuring us to kill "*tous ces salauds de Boches*" (all of these bastard Germans).

We passed through the 53rd and 54th Brigades, now on their objectives awaiting the leap-frogging of the 55th Brigade, and went on up the straight narrow drive, flanked by tall trees with, here and there, great clearings and piles of wood cut down by the Germans.

We had not met a single German so far, and having had a free hand from Irwin, I saw no sense in fruitlessly stopping where we were, to await our infantry. When we must have been five or six miles in front of our troops, we emerged from the trees into a large clearing. Owing to the position and narrowness of the strip of Triplex glass in front of us, I could see nothing whatever without impeding the view of the driver on my right.

Suddenly, without warning, bedlam seemed to have been let loose. Both the machine guns above and behind me had gone into action. Our car stopped. The guns blazed away, and I heard a new queer noise, rather like the sound of hailstones on metal, considerably magnified. It came from the bullets from a German machine gun glancing off our car, without causing the slightest damage, except to the grey paint. I peered cautiously through the Triplex glass, wondering vaguely whether it was guaranteed to be bullet proof, and what would happen if it was not. All I could see was something sticking up into the air fairly close to us, and some men, obviously Huns, legging it for all they were worth towards the trees in the distance. All the time the racket had been deafening, but a minute or so after we had opened fire it became even more ear-splitting. Smith's car behind mine had come up and his machineguns were joining in. Six or seven minutes later, the noise of the hailstones ceased. One by one the four guns from our cars ceased fire, and I poked my head cautiously out of the door of the car to see what had been going on.

A very remarkable and heartening sight it was; there were some 15 or 20 dead Germans lying in various positions, some grouped round an abandoned machine gun. The object I had seen sticking up into the air was the barrel of a large German artillery gun, possibly eight-inches or more in calibre. I had no time to examine it. If this gun had been fired at us we should have been blown to bits, but, luckily for us, we had been far too close to be shot at. There was no sign of any tractor for the gun. It might well have needed 10 or 12 horses to move it. If the Germans had used horses, there was no sign of them.

Our cars had arrived at the moment when a large body of men, possibly 100, had been trying to manhandle it from its muddy position in the clearing on to the road. The gun position had been defended by the machinegun whose crew had done their best. Unfortunately for them, thanks to the strength of our armour, all they could do was to scrape some of the paint off our cars. After losing several men, and realising the futility of their efforts, the survivors, like sensible men, had bolted to safety.

After this success, gained at no cost whatever to ourselves, there was no holding our men, not that I had slightest inclination to do so, and off we went again down the ride to find some more Germans. Then came frustration. The surface of the road, a mile or so beyond the gun position, was extremely slippery. My car skidded owing to the speed that the driver, in his excitement, was cramming on, and we found ourselves in the ditch. No one was hurt, but the steering column was bent and there was other minor damage. Smith's car pulled up behind us. He at once saw what was wrong and asked me what I intended to do. I had been considering this problem; I might tell him to go ahead alone in his car, no doubt to his great delight, to do as much damage as possible to any German forces he happened to meet. In that case I and the men in my car would be left sitting in the ditch and we should have been entirely helpless, unless we had removed our guns and ammunition to positions well away from the car, because the latter had landed in such a position in the ditch that there was no field of fire for the guns. Those German soldiers had been a stout-hearted lot, and it might well be that they, hearing nothing more, might conclude that both our cars had gone on eastwards, and come back in the hope of getting their great gun away, somehow or other. In this case we should have found ourselves in an extremely ignominious and dangerous position and, after all, we were well ahead of the final objective, and had justified our existence with a fair amount of success. So I said: "I don't want to spoil your fun, but, as far as I am concerned, orders should be 'Home James, and don't spare the horses.'" He fully agreed that this was the proper course.

I and the rest of the men in my car scrambled on to Smith's car, some inside, some on the roof and one or two round the bonnet. It would have been quite impossible to turn the car in that narrow, straight, muddy ride, so the lever was pulled, the back driver took over the steering, and we moved off again, this time towards the west. We saw no Germans at all. We passed the division's final objective line, and sometime later encountered the men of the 55th Brigade advancing towards it. The car was stopped. Everyone put their heads out and a good deal of ribaldry was exchanged. We told them that we had won their objective for them, and that all they had to do now was to walk there.

Then we went on our way until we encountered the staff of our brigade headquarters and I reported our adventures in the forest. Irwin seemed to be very pleased; as well he might be since the 55th Brigade, on the first occasion in which he commanded it, had reached its final objectives without a casualty. He thanked Smith warmly for the assistance rendered by him and his cars to the brigade, and told him he could return to Fourth Army headquarters. Smith and I took leave of each other with mutual expressions of regard, and told each other how much we had enjoyed ourselves, which was perfectly true. Later on, I had to make a written report of the action, in which I warmly commended young Smith, and I heard subsequently, to my great pleasure, that he had been awarded an M.C. I never saw him again. He was a very fine boy.

That evening the 18th (Eastern) Division was "squeezed out" of the line, according to the plan of attack. Other troops continued the pursuit of the enemy, and on 11 November, five days later, came the news of the Armistice, which, was received with complete calm. As a small item of interest, a radio apparatus, the first I had ever seen, was sent to our divisional headquarters and it was a novel experience to have message after message arriving from this source. The Germans, as ever and never happy without a grievance, were grumbling away because, according to them, one of our guns had continued to fire at them after 11.00 a.m.!

Printed in Great Britain
by Amazon